BEHIND THE MAGIC
50 YEARS OF
Disneyland®

Karal Ann Marling

with Donna R. Braden

The Henry Ford | Dearborn, Michigan

This book accompanies the exhibition *Behind the Magic—50 Years of Disneyland* organized by The Henry Ford in cooperation with Walt Disney Imagineering.

The Henry Ford gratefully acknowledges the extraordinary cooperation provided by Walt Disney Imagineering in the preparation of this exhibition.

The Henry Ford also thanks Karal Ann Marling and Donna R. Braden for the research they compiled and the insights they provided while writing the text, captions and sidebars for this publication.

The Henry Ford, located in Dearborn, Michigan, was founded in 1929 by automotive pioneer Henry Ford. This multi-venue destination includes Henry Ford Museum®, Greenfield Village®, The Henry Ford IMAX® Theatre, The Benson Ford Research Center™, and The Ford Rouge Factory Tour. The Henry Ford, America's Greatest History Attraction, provides unique educational experiences based on authentic objects, stories and lives from America's traditions of ingenuity, resourcefulness and innovation. Our purpose is to inspire people to learn from these traditions to help shape a better future.

Walt Disney Imagineering is the unique innovative organization that creates—from concept through construction—all Disney theme parks, resorts, attractions, cruise ships, real estate developments, and regional entertainment venues worldwide. Created in 1952 by Walt Disney, Imagineering's unique strength comes from the teamwork and syntheses of more than 1,400 creative and technical professionals representing more than 140 diverse disciplines.

Foreword

Steven K. Hamp
President, The Henry Ford

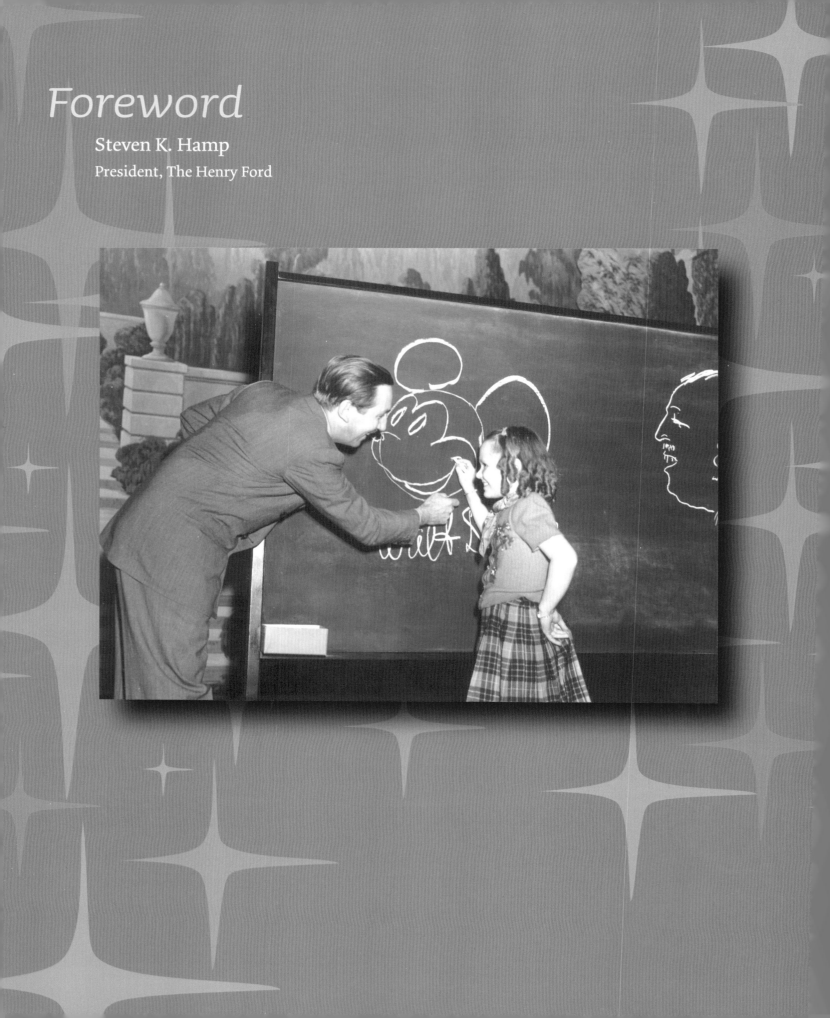

Both American originals, Henry Ford and Walt Disney had great admiration for each other. Although different in many ways, they shared one vital trait—exceptional and original vision. Once their own visions took shape, they became powerful and tenacious innovators in their pursuit. Ford's vision centered on a new way to think about the automobile. He landed on the idea of a cheap, readily accessible and easily operable car for the mass market, as opposed to the reigning paradigm of complex and expensive vehicles for a small, wealthy elite. His vision took shape as the durable Model T, a car that once claimed more than fifty percent of the automotive market. The achievement of his dream required a steady stream of innovations, some borrowed, some utterly novel: mass production, the moving assembly line, the $5 day for workers, total vertical integration of the manufacturing process, a bare-bones vehicle that got cheaper every year as the market got larger, and any color as long as it was black.

Walt Disney's vision, built on a highly successful cartoon and film career topped with Mickey's famous ears, was rooted in a new kind of mass entertainment for families. Created with equal measures of fantasy and myth, history and legend, and fun and education, his grand innovation was Disneyland, which, like the Model T, was truly something new under the sun. Disney's fantasy park drew upon a deep knowledge of American amusement and leisure-time precedent formatted in a totally original and completely immersive environment, and shaped by a genuine love of fun and an intuitive genius for understanding the popular mythology of the American psyche.

Disneyland and the Model T both left indelible marks on the 20th century. Their authors were entrepreneurs whose names had—and still have—global recognition. Their prime innovations, which to lesser minds seem obvious after their introduction, were both aimed at one of American democracy's greatest achievements—the growing

and optimistic middle class. Ford's humble "T" and Disney's fantasy world received plenty of high-brow vitriol, yet both hit a sweet spot with the American public to such an obvious extent as to cast their detractors as out-of-touch elitists.

It is not surprising, then, to learn that the creative genius of Henry Ford played a role in the development of Disneyland. But the link was not with Ford's Model T. Instead, Walt Disney came under the spell of Henry Ford's novel foray into the world of American history. Partly out of the extension of a billionaire's collecting passion and partly in response to a media portrayal of him as naïve and anti-intellectual, Ford set out to make a new kind of history museum in the mid-1920s. He wanted his museum to set forth American life "as it was lived," and to do so he focused on the concept of America's inventive genius. From humble inventions like the mechanical apple peeler to Thomas Edison's entire Menlo Park "invention factory," Ford initiated an acquisition frenzy that resulted in train-car loads of American artifacts arriving at his Dearborn, Michigan, automotive empire. From the dozens of historical structures and hundreds of thousands of objects he collected, Ford created The Edison Institute Museum and Greenfield Village, now called The Henry Ford, America's greatest history attraction.

Walt Disney visited Ford's history museum complex twice, in 1940 and again in 1948. Both visits are captured in tintype images, one of the 19th-century technologies available for visitors to explore in Greenfield Village at that time. During both visits, one suspects that Walt was gathering, consciously or unconsciously, grist for the mill that would eventually produce Disneyland.

Several of us from The Henry Ford recently had the great good fortune to visit Walt Disney Imagineering, the creative nerve center that provides the magic for Disneyland and the other Disney parks. Led by Marty Sklar, the quiet, unassuming and legendary force behind the Imagineers, this team not only creates the art, design and mechanics that make everything go, but they also preside over a fascinating historical archive of their work going back to the birth of Disneyland. Marty knew the link between Disney and Ford and between Disneyland and Greenfield Village, and it was Marty who was instrumental in bringing the two institutions together again. The result was an idea to create an exhibition celebrating Walt's creation and its cultural impact on the occasion of Disneyland's 50th anniversary. *Behind the Magic—50 Years of Disneyland* continues an episodic and unconventional relationship that started in 1940 with Walt's first trip to Dearborn.

During our visit to Walt Disney Imagineering, a wonderful bit of symmetry presented itself. We were shown the original sketch of an imagined Disneyland, cranked out over one incredibly intensive weekend by artist Herb Ryman as Walt stood over his shoulder. This magnificent rendering, at the very center of esoteric Disney lore, secured the New York financing needed for Walt's dream to see daylight. As it was carefully revealed, a delighted smile united the faces of the team from The Henry Ford. Distinctive and unique, new and utterly enticing, unmistakably the Disneyland we all came to know, the Ryman schematic drawing that became Disneyland nevertheless

During Walt's tour of Greenfield Village on April 12, 1940, he was said to have shown "great interest in everything mechanical, examining engines and old automobiles closely." After his tour, he posed for this old-fashioned tintype (opposite, above).

After an exciting and inspirational trip to the Chicago Railroad Fair in 1948, Walt Disney returned to Greenfield Village—this time with animator and fellow railroad enthusiast Ward Kimball. During their visit, they struck this formal pose at the tintype studio, choosing props from those that were available there (opposite, below).

A Pictorial Map of
EDISON INSTITUTE
MUSEUM & HISTORICAL
GREENFIELD VILLAGE
LOCATED AT DEARBORN, MICHIGAN
FOUNDED BY HENRY FORD
OPEN TO THE PUBLIC

Two trips to Greenfield Village helped inspire Walt to create Disneyland. Henry Ford's idealized American village is shown in this early pictorial view from 1934. Perhaps taking a cue from Disneyland much later, a perimeter railroad was added to Greenfield Village in 1972.

revealed an obvious genealogical relationship to Greenfield Village, like meeting a distant but familiar relative. Walt's last visit to Greenfield Village was in 1948; Ryman's sketch was produced in 1953, guided by the non-stop imaginative direction of the master himself. Although only one of undoubtedly many influences, Ford's historical village found expression in Ryman's work and, ultimately, in Disneyland. Disneyland features, among other things, a main street town feel, an encircling railroad, and a lagoon around which a steamboat chugs, all elements found in Greenfield Village. When we recently completely restored Greenfield Village, we took a page from Disneyland in street layout, traffic flow and thematic districts.

My guess is that Walt Disney would be happy to know that The Henry Ford is producing a historical exhibition on his grand and justly famous enterprise. I also believe Henry Ford would have been proud to know that his own beloved Greenfield Village influenced the design and development of Disneyland. Reciprocity is a wonderful thing, especially when it links and re-links the creative work of two of the 20th century's most visionary and entrepreneurial minds. ✦

Although previous artists' sketches laid much of the groundwork for what Disneyland would become, Walt felt that he needed a huge and fantastically detailed rendering to sell his ideas to the New York financiers. So he called upon Herb Ryman, one of his favorite artists, for help. Over the course of a September weekend in 1953—the legendary Lost Weekend—Walt described his vision as Ryman feverishly sketched away. Early Monday morning, Walt's brother, Roy, flew to New York with the drawing in hand and, along with the promise of a weekly TV show, secured funding from ABC TV!

Introduction

Martin A. Sklar

Vice Chairman and Principal Creative Executive, Walt Disney Imagineering

Front cover of The Story of Disneyland, *1955*

At The Walt Disney Company, we like to say that when families gather at one of our parks and resorts around the world, "Magic Happens." That's exactly what we knew would happen when two great "family institutions" came together to create this one-of-a-kind exhibition. We think you will agree that this event is extraordinary precisely because of the creative partnership between The Henry Ford and Walt Disney Imagineering.

Of course, from the moment we pried open the storage vault in search of just the right items for this exhibition, magic did happen. It was all there in thousands of artifacts, millions of photographs (Kodak says 4 percent of all photographs taken in America are shot in a Disney park!), and billions of memories treasured by the more than 500 million visitors who have made Disneyland the international symbol of "family fun."

Fifty years ago, Disneyland opened its gates for the first time on July 17, 1955. At its dedication, during the largest live television production ever aired, Walt Disney made a promise that has driven the Imagineers to create new magic ever since. *"Disneyland will never be completed,"* he told millions of television viewers, *"as long as there is imagination left in the world."*

Walt Disney's optimism for the future, and his unstinting drive to make Disneyland a "happy place...where parents and children can have fun — together," has spread all over the world to ten more Disney parks in Florida, Paris, Tokyo and (just opened in September 2005) in Hong Kong, China. Today, the sun never sets on the family fun at a Disney park somewhere in the world.

I started my Disney career at Disneyland one month before Disneyland opened on July 17, 1955. Some of my earliest learning moments were provided by the guests themselves. During the first summer, I listened to what they asked the ticket sellers. A frequent statement: "We want to go on the Jungle Cruise, The Flight to the Moon and

The Mark Twain Riverboat…but we don't want to go on any of the rides." We pondered this one, and finally figured it out: "rides" were the whips and shoot-the-chutes and twirling whirl-a-ways associated with the old, dying amusement parks. Disneyland, even the earliest guests realized, was something *different*. Our solution: strike the word "rides": we invented our own "Disneyland Dictionary" of *attractions, adventures and experiences*…a distinction that expressed Walt's vision to tell stories in three dimensions.

As the most "veteran" active Disney Imagineer, I'm often asked two questions:

First, what would Walt think about what has happened to his Magic Kingdom? I always respond that Walt's answer would be, "What took you so long?" It's not that Walt Disney was that impatient. Rather, he believed so strongly in what Disneyland represents that he was willing to mortgage a home and finance some of its earliest attractions personally. And it was his concept (he actually drew the first master plan himself) that set the creation of Florida's Walt Disney World in motion.

Second, why has the Disneyland idea been so successful around the world? The simple answer is that Walt Disney was right: there really was a pent-up need for things that parents and children can do, together. As Walt was fond of saying, "Adults are only kids grown up." But in my view, the success of the Disney parks and resorts has touched a much deeper nerve everywhere, from Anaheim to Hong Kong.

Walt Disney believed that things *can* be orderly and clean, that the people who host you and serve you *can* be friendly and caring, that you *can* speak to strangers in a public place, that

Walt and Herb Ryman discuss the Ford Pavilion's "Magic Skyway" show for the 1964 New York World's Fair.

the visual conflicts and contradictions found in our cities *can* be eliminated. This was the optimism and belief in a better future that Walt communicated and stood for. All of these things, standing as stark contrasts to much of what we find in our city and community experiences, are the experiences that *reassure* us—even for only the few hours we spend in a Disney park —that we can provide a better, more orderly and safer world for our families. We leave a Disney park *reassured*. We have opened our eyes to the world of the possible. We have *experienced* that better world.

Walt converses with cast member on Main Street.

And by the way, we had *fun* while we were being entertained, and "reassured."

Proving once again that "it's a small world, after all," the Walt Disney parks and resorts are in the midst of what we have christened "The Happiest Celebration on Earth." Together with The Henry Ford, we in the Disney organization are very proud to invite you to step inside the curtains and experience *"Behind the Magic—50 Years of Disneyland."* ✦

"To All Who Come to This Happy Place...Welcome!"

Welcome DISNEYLAND

We hope you will have fun here, and that this souv will long recall happy, carefree hours in a place d cated to your enjoyment.

The first edition illustrations on these pages s buildings and exhibits in artist rendering stage. T was so we could have the booklet ready for our e visitors. But DISNEYLAND will always be build and growing and adding new things...new way having fun, of learning things and sharing the m exciting adventures which may be experienced her the company of family and friends.

What you see in DISNEYLAND represents combined efforts of hundreds of artists, architects, entists, expert craftsmen and engineers who have he us carry out a long cherished dream.

The park-playground fulfills a wish that thos us who like the same things might more closely s the pleasures I have had in exploring the paths of f and folklore, of nature and science and historical leg on the screen and television.

So, the opening of DISNEYLAND, where visi of every age and circumstance can learn joyously f fact and live closely with fantasy, has been for m as I hope it has been for you—a most happy even dream come true.

Walt Disne

July 17, 1955—the date that went down in history as the historic opening of Walt Disney's new attraction in a former orange grove in Anaheim, California. Afterwards, they called it "Black Sunday." It was so hot in Orange County that the new-laid asphalt pavement melted: the lady-visitors—who turned out, of course, in hats and high heels because this was an important *occasion!*—found themselves stuck to the bridge leading toward the big, wedding-cake of a fairy-tale castle that loomed over a collection of cute little buildings, enormous crowds, and movie stars scattered across the 60-acre plot.

A hundred additional acres were given over to what may have been the nation's largest parking lot. With a 12,000-car capacity (at 25¢ per vehicle), the lot also made a statement about Mr. Disney's "Disneyland." In the golden age of postwar automobility, Disneyland was to be a place for walking, for enjoying the scenery close up, at eye level—for stopping here and there to sit in a sidewalk café or to watch an old-time blacksmith shoe his horse. It was no place for Detroit's latest two-tone tail-fin family chariot.

On that particular Sunday, however, Disneyland was a mess. The pavement oozed and plopped. There weren't enough drinking fountains; was this a conspiracy

---

THE STORY OF Disneyland

Disneyland is living proof that dreams do come true. For twenty years, Walt Disney dreamed of creating "a fabulous playground…a showplace of magic and living facts…a place for people to find happiness and knowledge." Disneyland is the realization of Walt's dream and, through it, he has not only made his own dream come true, but he has brought to life, for millions of others, the fun and fantasies of childhood.

With the heady scent of orange blossoms from the surrounding groves filling the air, you enter the gates of Disneyland and leave day to day reality behind. The terraced embankment which completely encloses Disneyland was designed to keep the outside world from intruding upon you. Here, you are in a kingdom set apart.

Although Disneyland covers an area of 160 acres, you need walk only 1¼ miles in order to see it all. And no matter where you might be when thirst or the pangs of hunger strike, you will find that food and refreshment are always close at hand. There is an abundance of restaurants devoted to pleasing all tastes and all budgets, from the unique Buffeteria for a quick snack to the re-creation of early century elegance in a Delmonico-style cafe.

But dreams do not come true overnight. It took years of work by many men to bring the idea to realization. The total in time, effort, and talent devoted to this project is

©Copyright, 1955 by Disneyland, Incorporated. All rights reserved throughout the world. Printed in U.S.A. Designed and produced by Western Printing & Lithographing Company.

Spread from The Story of Disneyland, *1955*

to sell more Coca-Cola? The hot dogs and the popcorn ran out. And where were the restrooms? Company publicists had issued twenty thousand tickets to the official Dedication Day to reporters, local dignitaries, corporate investors and prominent faces in the Hollywood film colony. But some would-be guests forged their own passes. A stretch of make-believe jungle along Harbor Boulevard soon became a favorite entry spot for determined fans without V.I.P. credentials.

By means fair and foul, some 30,000 people were packed inside the park's berm by midmorning, with more to come. The earthen berm or barrier (the miniature railroad ran along the top) was

Opening Day bedlam: The first guests to cross the drawbridge into Fantasyland (below). Long lines of guests wait to get into Tomorrowland (right).

supposed to seal off this "happy place" from the burdensome cares of the outside world. Once inside the park, the tourist was forced to forget the snarl of traffic on the Santa Ana Freeway, which had vanished from view. The car, currently baking outside in the "Dopey" section of the parking lot, was no longer visible either, once Mom and Dad and Sis and Junior had passed through the Disneyland turnstile.

Walt prepares to read the Fantasyland dedication in front of the TV cameras on Opening Day.

Inside the berm that Sunday, the crowds swelled. Long lines formed at all the rides. The next day, a gas leak threatened to close down the largest section of the grounds. Even worse, with mere minutes to go before his televised dedication speech, Walt Disney was nowhere to be found. The nervous proprietor (who had spent the night in the park) turned up just in time. A balky door had trapped him momentarily in his little apartment up above the Gay Nineties fire station on Main Street, not fifty feet from the spot where he was supposed to welcome the world to his greatest dream come true.

Artist, entrepreneur, certified genius and America's most beloved entertainer, the avuncular Disney finally took his place at the microphone and began. "Disneyland is your land," he announced in his flat Midwestern accent. "Here, age relives fond memories of the past, and here youth may savor the challenge and promise of the future. Disneyland is dedicated to the ideals, the dreams, and hard facts that have created America…with the hope that it will be a source of joy and inspiration to all the world."

The *real* opening day—when anybody could come who paid the admission fees—$1 for grownups and a mere 50¢ for kids; rides or "attractions" were extra—was almost worse. By 2:00 A.M., the state police had begun to notice the volume of cars building on the highways around Anaheim. By 8:00 A.M., two hours before the start

Welcome to Disneyland

This is your personal map for the Kingdom of Happiness — Walt Disney's Magic Kingdom — Disneyland.

This is the kingdom that was created for *YOU* — and your personal happiness.

All of us — Disneyland's Hosts and Hostesses — are dedicated to making your first — and subsequent visits — a very pleasant and treasured experience.

Disneyland was created and designed as a new concept in family entertainment — something for everyone, of every age. Here is the world of Tomorrow, and Yesterday — Fantasy and Adventure skillfully blended in every detail for your pleasure and enjoyment.

As Disneylander's we are proud to play a part in creating happiness for you and your family. Whatever we can do to make this visit more enjoyable — won't you please let us help you.

© Copyright, 1955, by Disneyland, Inc.

Map of Disneyland from
Opening Day, July 17, 1955

DISNEYLAND

TO ALL WHO COME TO THIS HAPPY PLACE

Welcome

Disneyland is your land. Here age relives fond memories of the past . . . and here youth may savor the challenge and promise of the future.

Disneyland is dedicated to the ideals, the dreams, and the hard facts that have created America . . . with the hope that it will be a source of joy and inspiration to all the world.

July 17, 1955

(Official dedication plaque located at flagpole in Town Square on Main Street)

neyland

Your Personal Guide to Disneyland

There are five main areas in Disneyland, and several other important features which you can locate handily by referring to this map. Study the attached legend for a more enjoyable visit to this Magic Kingdom: **1.** Main Entrance and Exit **2.** Town Square **3.** Main Street **4.** The Plaza **5.** Adventureland **6.** Frontierland **7.** Fantasyland **8.** Tomorrowland.

NOTE ALSO THE FOLLOWING PERSONAL SERVICES WHICH MAY BE LOCATED ON THE MAP BY THE LETTERS INDICATED BELOW

A. Lost children — A Headquarters for Lost Children and Parents is maintained at City Hall in Town Square. It is staffed by experienced attendants who maintain a special playground for the youngsters. If your child becomes lost, call directly at City Hall.

First Aid — A complete First Aid Station is located in the City Hall on Town Square. A doctor and registered nurses are always in attendance.

Security — Security Officers are stationed throughout Disneyland. The Headquarters is in the City Hall on Town Square.

B. Rest Rooms — There are women's and men's rest rooms on Main St. as well as in Frontierland, Fantasyland, Adventureland and Tomorrowland. They are easily identified by signs.

Take home this map and color it after your visit to Disneyland.

of business, 8,000 would-be customers were already in line and the giant parking lot was almost full. At 10:00 A.M., Walt Disney himself strolled up to the ticket booths and personally welcomed the first two children in line: little Christine Fess, age five, from North Hollywood, and her seven-year-old cousin, Michael Schwartner, of Bakersfield.

But once again, there were problems: a huge volume of trash, scattered everywhere; a riverboat that almost capsized when hordes of people raced up the gangplank and all stood on one side of the ship at the same time; chronic traffic tie-ups. Despite the glitches, Disneyland's customers—the "guests"—spoke with their dollars and quarters. Like Michael and Christine, they had a wonderful time. And they kept on coming. Walt Disney's "happy place" was a resounding success. In its first seven days of operation, paid attendance totaled 161,657.

There were critics, though. One disillusioned reporter resented the cost. "Walt's dream is a nightmare," he complained. "To me [the Park] felt like a giant cash register, clinking and clanging, as creatures of Disney magic came tumbling down from their lofty places in my daydreams to peddle their charms with the aggressiveness of so many curbside barkers." Late in July, the *New York Times*, too, took up the chorus of criticism about the cost of the extras, not included in the price of admission. Although Disney had invested $17 million in the venture, the press seemed resentful about paying for an additional ticket to ride in the cups and saucers of the Mad Hatter's tea party,

Walt Disney's "happy place" was a resounding success. In its first seven days of operation, paid attendance totaled 161,657.

however delightfully it had been brought to life in the park. A family of four could easily drop $100 in a day, journalists figured.

Opening Day fanfare in front of Sleeping Beauty Castle.

Was Disneyland, albeit bigger and better, simply an up-to-date movie-driven version of the old "tourist trap," in which costumed locals sat in cement replicas of big shoes or Peter's giant pumpkin copied from storybooks? Highways and cars bred Santa Claus villages and Gingerbread cottages to fleece unwary tourists with their overpriced souvenirs and ice cream cones. The *Times* went on to cite a $600,000 Storyland in New Jersey as a cheaper version of what Disney had accomplished in California, with a lot more hoopla. It was all a fad. It probably wouldn't last.

And yet here we are. Disneyland is fifty years old this year—one of the most famous landmarks in the world. Why? How is Disneyland different from all those defunct Santalands? Why do winning athletes and ordinary families and sick children and lots of smiling, unattached grown-ups want nothing more than a trip to Disneyland—or one of its farflung subsidiaries? Just what is Disneyland all about? ✦

2

Disneyland on TV

The opening of Disneyland was one of the great national events of the 1950s, thanks to the TV set, the latest ultra-modern appliance to take its place in the American home. Like Ike's inaugural in 1953, Nixon's infamous "Checkers" speech, Elvis Presley's startling appearance on "The Ed Sullivan Show," and the gala coronation of the young Elizabeth II, the program was one of those rare collective happenings that everybody watched on black-and-white television. The show was called "Dateline Disneyland."

ABC—the least prestigious of the three major networks—gave the Disneyland dedication ceremonies unprecedented live coverage. Twenty-four cameras (or 29, according to one reporter). Three famous TV hosts (Bob Cummings, Ronald Reagan and Art Linkletter). And an air of madcap spontaneity enhanced by a spate of "technical difficulties." Missed cues. Lost microphones. Inexplicable happenings. Every moment held a new surprise.

Fess Parker, who played "Davy Crockett" on Disney's weekly series (also called *Disneyland*), got lost in the off-camera foliage of Frontierland when he was supposed to be charming the at-home audience. Irene Dunne, the queen mother of the movie colony, showered Linkletter with shards of glass when she tried to christen a Disneyland riverboat for the camera. While the voice-over commentary was describing the gala arrival of Cinderella's coach, the grainy image on the small screen showed Western stars Roy Rogers and Dale Evans instead. Walt Disney turned up early for some of his on-camera dialogue—and could be heard wondering out loud how things were going. Or he was late and popped into the

Television sensation Davy Crockett (played by Fess Parker) joins Walt on a ride down Main Street.

picture breathless and agitated. The glitches were part of the fun. All in all, "Dateline Disneyland" was a terrific success.

This was as it should be, because Disneyland—the place—was literally a park that was also a TV show. Walt Disney, unlike his fellow movie moguls, was willing to take a chance on the TV set in the living room. Hollywood feared that television would kill off the traditional Friday night at the movies. Disney, on the other hand, saw great possibilities for studios willing to design shows of their own for a stay-at-home TV audience. As early as 1950, in a "special" sponsored by Coca-Cola and aired on sixty-two stations on Christmas Day, Disney entertained America's families with a preview of *Alice in Wonderland*, an animated feature soon to open at neighborhood theaters everywhere. As one clear-eyed observer noted, "That telecast should be worth $1 million at the box office...." And so it was. Television sold movies. And there was every reason to believe that it could sell something called a "theme park."

Hollywood feared that television would kill off the traditional Friday night at the movies. Disney, on the other hand, saw great possibilities for studios willing to design shows of their own for a stay-at-home TV audience.

Walt pointing out to TV viewers how each of the "lands" in his new Park will look.

For almost a decade, Walt Disney had been dickering with ideas to create something more tangible than a cartoon, and less fixed in form. A place. A glorious playground. When *Snow White*, was finished, he sadly noted, it was truly finished. If this scene or that one could have been done differently, well, it was too late now. But with this kind of park—you could fiddle with it, see what worked and what didn't. Watch the trees grow tall. Dream up new delights. Tinker. Fix it up. To use Walt's own self-invented word, you could "plus" things and make 'em better, forever!

In the meantime, he contented himself with building steam trains in his own backyard and mechanical devices that controlled tiny figures moving through scenery like tireless, robotic actors—or animated characters in three dimensions. Making miniatures gave Walt Disney a welcome sense of being able to produce something tangible with his own two hands. In common with other corporate paper-pushers of the

In 1954, Disney artist Peter Ellenshaw created this vast bird's-eye of the park for Walt's presentation of the concept on his Wednesday night show for ABC TV.

postwar era, he was frustrated by his detachment from the fruits of increasingly abstract labors. He couldn't even sign his own name properly any more, in the curlicues that had become the corporate logo of a sprawling film empire! Crafting tiny furniture and figures, on the other hand, provided a feeling of solid, observable accomplishment. And the process of miniaturization itself put the creator in firm control of *something*—if not a sprawling company, then of his own world.

For a time, Disney thought of sending these box-like constructions of his—they looked just like TV sets tuned to a Disney show—on tour around the country, in an old railroad car: put a dime in the slot and see the characters dance! The idea was quickly shelved, however, plagued from the beginning by balky machinery and crushing expense. So ended "Disneylandia," the first Disneyland of the imagination.

Others soon followed. Throughout the 1940s and early '50s, Walt considered plans for a small park on the

Walt's childhood memories of Marceline, Missouri (below, top), inspired his creation of Disneyland's Main Street. But as the model shows (below, bottom), Walt "cleaned up" the streetscape—designing the buildings to the same era and scaling the whole thing down to give guests a friendly, child's-eye view of the past.

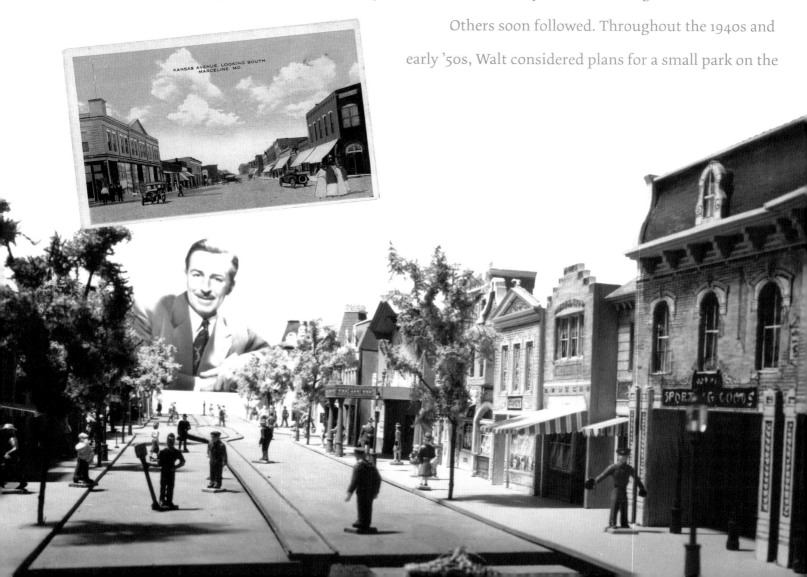

"The format of the show is America," Walt wrote in a memo to his staff. "We can mingle fantasy, we can dream and be fantastic. There is no one over here telling us that we cannot—I think this is part of America."

site of one of the studio parking lots. Should there be statues of Mickey and the rest of the Disney cartoon stars? Or a more ambitious effort, with a train to ride and a town and an Indian Village? By 1948, Walt had begun serious research on his dream-in-the-making with visits to Henry Ford's Greenfield Village and the Chicago Railroad Fair. He came back enthralled with the notion of a sort of living history museum, with a variety of distinct eras and locales, people in costumes, appropriate foodstuffs and souvenirs. Disney being Disney, of course, his park would also be a lot of fun for kids (and the adults who came with them).

In September of 1953, Walt summoned Herb Ryman to the Studio and prepared to keep him there all weekend. It was crunch time. Walt's brother Roy was going to New York to negotiate a television contract with the Big Three. A hit show could sell this Disney park to America at large. Or generate the revenue to get it up and running. But how to explain a "theme park" to people who had never heard of one, for the very good reason that Walt Disney was inventing it on the spot? That's where Ryman came in. Walt talked. Herbie drew. A castle right in the middle. Separate realms for glimpses of the past and the future, the exotic third world, the imaginative realm of the fairy tale. And a Main Street just like the one Walt and Roy remembered fondly from growing up on a farm in Marceline, Missouri.

Timing is Everything

Disneyland's huge success was not a coincidence. American society was rapidly changing after World War II, and Walt's vision capitalized on these changes. Aimed directly at new post-war suburban families, Disneyland shrewdly promised both an escape from and a confirmation of their lifestyles. The lure was irresistible.

Baby boom families were the largest and fastest growing demographic group in the country, and the suburbs seemed perfectly made for them. During the 1950s, 83 percent of the total population growth in America was in the suburbs. The families that could afford a home in the "New Suburbia" also had the desire to spend time together, the money to buy things beyond the basic necessities (like TVs) and the luxury of leisure time.

New suburban families also purchased cars in unprecedented numbers. The number of two-car families actually doubled between 1951 and 1958. This second car often became the family car, perfect for outings and those two-week vacations now guaranteed many workers. A family car trip offered freedom and escape from the pressures of daily life, an adventure into the unknown and a chance to explore the country. Coinciding with this explosion in car ownership, roads improved dramatically. Highways became wider and straighter, and the first sections of the new American interstate freeway system were completed.

Disneyland couldn't have been more perfectly situated than in California. "The Golden State" had long been considered a land of dreams and promise—by everyone from early explorers and gold seekers to Hollywood producers and Dust Bowl migrants. For vacationers heading Out West, California was a land blessed with a mild climate, awe-inspiring scenery and abundant good roads. In 1957, a hefty 40 percent of visitors came to Disneyland from outside California.

Meanwhile, Los Angeles witnessed its own postwar boom, as the lure of sunshine, good health and job opportunities drew thousands of young families and turned the city into a sprawling metropolis. Walt cleverly located Disneyland in the rapidly growing suburban area of Anaheim, with its easy access to an evolving network of expressways.

A 1956 souvenir postcard showing the Los Angeles expressway system. How quickly and efficiently that traffic is moving!

A family enjoys time together watching their new television in this 1951 Motorola advertisement from Woman's Home Companion.

In this 1953 Ford Motor Company advertisement, the kids proudly photograph the family's new automobile, with Mom, Dad and their suburban ranch house in the background.

The drawing drew yawns at NBC and CBS. Amusement parks were public nuisances, populated by lowlife—a blight on the community. At ABC, where a possible Disney show amounted to a gift from the gods of television, a deal was struck without delay. On April 2, 1954, it was announced that Walt Disney would create a new weekly show for the network. "The format of the show is America," Walt wrote in a memo to his staff. "We can mingle fantasy, we can dream and be fantastic. There is no one over here telling us that we cannot—I think this is part of America. We can show Frontierland and Main Street as part of that heritage." The name of the show was *Disneyland* and behind the scenes, the moneymen scrambled to draft an agreement whereby the network would bankroll a park of the same name.

And so it began. Every Wednesday night, the nation put aside homework and housework to watch the opening roll of *Disneyland*: four panels, introduced by Tinker Bell, describing four possible themes for that week's extravaganza. Would it

Closeup of Herb Ryman's 1953 sketch of Disneyland (see page 11), showing Main Street leading to the Hub, then off into the various lands.

be Adventureland? Frontierland (cue the Indian drums!)? Tomorrowland? Fantasyland? A shower of fairy dust—and there stood Walt himself, pointing to a huge map of his as-yet-unbuilt park, revealing models of its attractions, and, best of all, showing that each of Tinker Bell's TV lands was a real place where tourists could actually take a boat ride through the jungle, play at being Davy Crockett, fly over Neverland with Peter Pan, or blast into space with the astronauts of the future. In other words, it would soon be possible to walk right into a Walt Disney movie! Into Walt Disney's world!

Each week, the *Disneyland* show took up one of these subjects, or "lands," using the products of the Disney Studios to do so. On a Fantasyland night, for example, the audience might see clips from famous Disney animated films. While excerpts from *Alice in Wonderland* were being played on television, workmen out in Anaheim were busily constructing a set of madly revolving cups and saucers, based on the scene where Alice attends the Mad Hatter's tea party. On Frontierland night, the big attrac-

tion was the made-for-TV series based on the quasi-fictional life of Davy Crockett—a series so successful that it was recut as a feature movie and set off a fad for coonskin caps that threatened to drive furry animals into extinction. The park, like the *Disneyland* program, was a kind of biography of the works of Walt Disney, based on his live and animated movies, his documentary films, and his TV shows. The park, the host and the show were one and the same entity.

"Every time I'd get to thinking of television I would think of this Park," Walt later told a biographer. "So I just sort of insisted that my Disneyland Park be a part of my television show." In July of 1955, Disneyland became the world's first living TV set. ✦

Walt operates his miniature steam train, the Carolwood Pacific, in the backyard of his home in Holmby Hills, California (above).

Walt Disney waves cheerily to the Opening Day crowd as he approaches in the Santa Fe & Disneyland Railroad (below).

Walt Disney's wife, Lilly, attributed the creation of Disneyland to his lifelong love of trains. Indeed, one of the continual elements in all his plans for the Park is the steam train rolling around a perimeter track. Some of Walt's fondest boyhood memories centered around the excitement and adventure of trains. Even as an adult, he took trains whenever he traveled long distances. Story has it that his famed character Mickey Mouse was "born" on a train, as Walt traveled back home to California after a disappointing trip to New York City.

With the pressures of the studio getting to Walt during the 1940s, doctors suggested he take up a hobby. Turning to trains seemed a logical choice. Walt found that building and operating model trains not only gave him a sense of control but also let him travel back to the pleasant memories of his childhood. And in this he was not alone. A whole generation of men just like Walt, who had grown up during the glory days of trains, was recapturing these same memories by collecting, building and operating different-sized trains.

Among these train buffs was Walt's friend, animator Ward Kimball, who convinced him to attend the Chicago Railroad Fair in 1948—a turning point in Walt's thinking about his Park. When they returned home, he decided that he just had to build a large-scale miniature (1/8 of full-size) steam-driven train. He built and operated his Carolwood Pacific in the family's backyard (to his wife's dismay, although he appeased her by naming the locomotive after her, the Lilly Belle). When it came time to decide what kind of train should operate around Disneyland, Walt's choice was easy. He had the Lilly Belle from his backyard enlarged five times for the locomotive in the Park. Then he named his railroad the "Santa Fe" (& Disneyland) after the beloved train line of his youth. Santa Fe Railroad was also an early sponsor of the Disneyland steam trains.

3

Main Street USA

MAIN STREET, U.S.A.

The nostalgic charm of 1890 comes to life again in this accurate reproduction of Main Street in a typical American town. You will delight in the picturesque array of restaurants, amusements, and shops packed with distinctive merchandise, which line both sides of the street.

At the end of Main Street is the Plaza, the heart of Disneyland, from which its four fantastic "lands" reach out in all directions to worlds of enchantment and surprise.

Points of entry are crucial to any human experience, especially a new one. Scholars speak of that significant "liminal" moment when we cross out of one spatial/spiritual domain and into another. In the case of Disneyland, the key geographic fact is the passage from the real world of cars and free-ways and gas-station logos into a magi-cal space sealed away from the cares and preoccupations of everyday life. Disney's guests walked under the railroad tracks and into the America of circa 1900, just as the horse-drawn trolley was disap-pearing and Henry Ford's horseless car-riages were about to make their bow. Main Street USA, as this townscape was called, ran from the railroad station (and the berm) to the very heart of Disneyland. It introduced and defined the park's pleasures. It eased the transi-tion from Anaheim to make-believe. And Main Street USA drew upon one of the most cherished ideals of the 1950s: the concept of community, or, as

Spread from The Story of Disneyland, *1955*

McCall's magazine termed it in the Easter issue of 1954, "togetherness."

While raw suburban developments struggled with the problem of forging a coherent identity in Levittowns devoid of familiar civic institutions, the old-fashioned, neighborly small town acquired the luster of some half-forgotten paradise of white picket

fences, jolly merchants and piquant quirks of architecture. The movies had given wish-

ful form to that ideal during the tumultuous Depression years with the popular Andy

Board the
SANTA FE
& DISNEYLAND R.R.
at Main St.
Frontierland
or Fantasyland depots

SANTA FE & I

MAIN STREET

Hardy series, set in the town of Carvel, a visual model of Mid-

American perfection. The Bedford Falls of *It's a Wonderful Life* (1946)

and the Mandrake Falls of *Mr. Deeds Goes to Town* (1936), both

films by Frank Capra, preached the fundamental goodness and

honesty of little towns in out-of-the-way spots. In *Our Town* (1938),

playwright Thornton Wilder had used the passage of time in Grover's

Corners as a metaphor for the larger American cycle of life, death

and rebirth.

During the 1950s, in a diluted and often comedic way, the

backlot Main Street set came to television, with its charm almost

intact. The Andersons of *Father Knows Best* debuted in 1954, with all

the props of an Andy Hardy movie: the lawn, the shutters, the quirky cast of teachers, neighbors and local characters, all fundamentally benign and endearingly colorful. This was also the ethos of *The Adventures of Ozzie and Harriet*. Bankers, salesmen, cops and the ubiquitous guy-next-door populated a townscape of spit-and-polish orderliness. The community, and the family units of which it was composed, were the stars of the show on 1950s television, along with the scenery itself, as if to reassure the viewer that friendliness, gingerbread facades and gleaming front windows went together somehow in places that looked like Hollywood's version of Home Town America.

Walt Disney's Main Street USA, perhaps the most carefully sketched and rendered portion of Disneyland, reeked of nostalgia for a golden age. "I love the nostalgic, myself," Walt Disney remarked. "I hope we never lose some of the things of the past." In one sense, Main Street is what folk art critics call a "memory picture," depicting Disney's recollections of the main drag in Marceline, as seen by the wondering eyes of a little

This stretch of Main Street resembled the small towns where many of the early visitors to Disneyland were born. In a modern era, with little reverence for old buildings, the spit-and-polish perfection of Main Street USA would inspire a movement to preserve and restore Main Street architecture across the country.

boy who colored it with all the storybook hues of a Baghdad market out of the *Arabian Nights*. But the evidence provided by drawings made for Walt by studio artists in 1952 and 1953 suggests a more complicated provenance. One set of sketches clearly depicts the Old West atmosphere of Walter Knott's Ghost Town (1952), just down the road from Anaheim in Buena Park, California. Knott, the popularizer of the boysenberry, had put together a collection of derelict board-front buildings and railroad trains when the mining towns of Nevada and the other Western states were abandoned. He did so out of a passion for a bygone era in American history. But he was also seeking a way to entertain a long line of customers who had driven out to Orange County to enjoy one of Mrs. Knott's famous homemade chicken dinners (with boysenberry pie).

Another set of drawings reflects artist Harper Goff's reminiscences of growing up in Fort Collins, Colorado, where his father edited the local newspaper. Downtown Fort Collins is still a wonderfully preserved and highly eclectic ensemble of turn-of-the-century commercial buildings, albeit structures considerably larger than those on Walt Disney's Main Street. And unlike the Disneyland version, the preliminary "blue sky" visuals by Goff show Main Street as a long row of buildings that bleeds off into a residential neighborhood of churches and substantial homes with welcoming front porches.

Although the idea of putting visitors up in houses like those—a themed hotel?—seems to have been discussed briefly as Walt polished his plans for Disneyland, it was an impossible scheme to implement in 1954, with fewer than 257 days left between groundbreaking and televised dedication. In the end, however, the two short blocks of Walt Disney's commercial Main Street appealed so strongly to visitors because the place represented a collective memory. Main Street embodied everybody's recollections of small town USA—Knott's, Goff's, Disney's, and those of scores of others who looked back to the wonderful world of childhood, a time in life when the old home town or the old neighborhood seemed new, shiny, beautiful, mysterious and endlessly fascinating. Walt's three-dimensional dreamscape came straight out of the collective consciousness of America.

There were dissenting voices to be heard on the subject of Main Street as well. Sinclair Lewis, for example, had exposed the narrowness and aesthetic indifference of Gopher Prairie in his bestselling novel of 1920, a book titled *Main Street*.

Preliminary drawings for Main Street pictured a residential neighborhood which was never built. Main Street remained a tribute to the ideal of street-corner capitalism.

There's a Great Big Beautiful Tomorrow

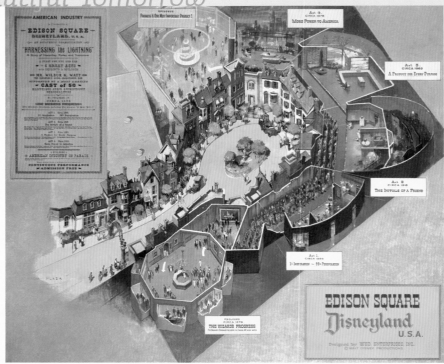

Today the well-loved Carousel of Progress show entertains guests at Walt Disney World in Florida. Guests are whisked around a central core of four scenes that reveal the changing lifestyle of a family since the 1890s. Each scene reinforces the notion that our lives have been improved by new technology. The premise of the show seems rather quaint and nostalgic in today's world, although the theme song sure is catchy!

Carousel of Progress actually owes its origins to a very early idea called Edison Square, an attraction that was to tell the story of progress through electricity. Designed as a rather urban-style street, it was situated off the Hub, between Main Street and Tomorrowland. On first glance, it looked like a neighborhood of townhouses from different American cities. The center of the traffic circle featured a statue of Thomas Edison, while electric street lamps dotting the street completed the scene. But the real scenes were behind these buildings, which—it turned out—were just facades for a series of sit-down shows and walk-through exhibits.

So how did Edison Square turn into the Carousel of Progress? It happened by way of the 1964 New York World's Fair. Walt convinced General Electric to fund "a unique show that would showcase the electrical industry and tell how it has helped the nation grow and prosper." Thus, the GE Pavilion at the World's Fair featured "Carousel of Progress," a show designed in a giant carousel, around which the audience would rotate, and brought to life with 32 Audio-Animatronics® figures. After the Fair, this show was moved to Disneyland and re-opened as the centerpiece of the newly re-designed Tomorrowland. The Carousel of Progress show ran there until 1973, when Disney staff felt that it had run its course and it was moved to Walt Disney World.

One additional note to this story. When Carousel of Progress opened at Disneyland, guests were invited after the show to ascend a "speed ramp" to a second floor, to view a huge working model of a real city of the future, called "Progress City." This was Walt's first concept for EPCOT—his Experimental Prototype Community of Tomorrow.

Original concept for Edison Square, circa 1954 (above). Old and new are juxtaposed in this show first developed for the 1964 New York World's Fair (left).

Sherwood Anderson, in *Winesburg, Ohio* (1919) reached the same conclusions. Yet paradoxically, by attacking the Midwestern town of the interregnum between the so-called "Gay Nineties" and World War I, the satirists only reinforced the importance of Main Streets to the life of the nation. Whether that central business corridor was to be found in Minnesota, Ohio, Missouri—or Anaheim, California—whether it was grand or a little seedy, it was the icon around which a definition of "home" coalesced in memory.

Having a single point of entry into Disneyland meant that everyone had to walk down Main Street together, in a great democratic ritual of collectivity. Many of those who took the walk were reluctant pedestrians in 1955. They lived in subdivisions without sidewalks. They commuted to work in distant cities. Their children went to school by bus. In one of the ironies that pepper his career, Walt Disney, by this audacious stroke of planning, insisted that the pleasures of walking through pleasant surroundings trumped a trip on the very freeways that brought his customers to Disneyland. And Main Street was only the beginning of the glorious alternatives to the family car presented in the course of a day at Disneyland. There were snorting trains, of course; a monorail; a steamboat; and eventually, a people-mover system, along with a full roster of let's-pretend vehicles, ranging from submarines to rocket ships. At every turn, Disneyland pointed out how American transportation systems could be better and more efficient by making them more fun.

The Main Street walk amounted to an assertion of control: there was no ready alternative. And ever since July of 1955, dissenting voices have charged Disney with being a sort of humbug, a Missouri-bred Wizard of Oz, orchestrating human activity from behind a curtain of benevolent fascism. But Walt Disney would never have denied the fact that he was directing the footsteps of guests, in order to create the illusion that separates his "theme park" from the run-of-the-mill amusement park. At Disneyland,

Crowds making their way down Main Street on Opening Day.

Main Street USA drew upon one of the most cherished ideals of the 1950s: the concept of community, or, as McCall's magazine termed it in the Easter issue of 1954, "togetherness."

the family that walked down Main Street USA (always impeccably clean, of course, as it was in Hollywood films) was also walking into a movie, of which they were the stars. Scene One: the railroad station and the adjacent square in front of City Hall. Scene Two: the Plaza off yonder, where Main Street almost imperceptibly fades into the central Hub, from which the other lands radiate. Main Street is the scenery in that internal movie, the stage set, the backlot upon which each of us can reenact our own hometown dramas—whether or not we ever lived in such a place as this.

In his ad-libbed commentary on the peripheral railroad during the opening moments of "Dateline Disneyland," Art Linkletter mentions that the Disney train was built to 5/8 scale—and so it was. This figure gave rise to the "urban legend" that Main Street, too, was constructed according to a model railroader's rigid adherence to a certain gauge or size, relative to the real thing. But the storefronts of Main Street are not formulaic in any respect. The ground floors—the doors, the show windows—were built to human scale, since the intent was to encourage the actor/guest to enter these spaces. As the eye moves up the buildings, however, the second and third stories shrink steadily. Bricks and stones and boards sometimes become smaller, too, as the structures rise to meet the sky. This set decorator's trick is called "forced perspective."

On Main Street, forced perspective seems to have been achieved through artistic approximation. Did the Emporium look right? The Swift's Market? In the end, the ad hoc

Walt thoughtfully looks on as guests enter Disneyland.

Give Me Liberty...Or Not

In 1956, Walt's Imagineers began work on a "patriotic attraction" just off Main Street. Liberty Street—as it came to be called—would take guests into the heart of the Revolutionary Era of the late 1700s. The street would feature architecture from each of the thirteen original colonies, as well as craft shops with artisans (like blacksmiths, silversmiths and glassblowers) who would demonstrate and sell their wares (right, above).

The street led to a grand re-creation of Independence Hall, where the "Liberty Bell would be constantly tolling." Inside guests would find the main attraction— the Hall of Presidents—a theatrical presentation in which all of America's presidents came to life to present "the mighty cavalcade of American history." Each president would be life-size, dimensional and fully animated through the magic of Audio-Animatronics® technology. As early as 1960, actual recordings of scripts for this show were made, under Walt Disney's direct supervision.

Whatever became of Liberty Street? As so often happened in those early days, other projects took precedence. But a good idea always found its way back to the surface. The ideas and technology created for this show led to Disney's "Great Moments with Mr. Lincoln" show at the 1964 New York World's Fair (right, middle), and eventually led to Liberty Square and the Hall of Presidents at Walt Disney World in Florida.

Audio-Animatronics® Mr. Lincoln performing on stage (right). Imagineer Blaine Gibson (far right) sculpts the final touches to Mr. Lincoln's head—before the Audio-Animatronics® figure is created.

tinkering with size gives the illusion of reality, with a twist. While the street suggests a trip into history, the space is still small: comfy, cozy, almost domestic in feeling—like a cross between a dollhouse and a one-story suburban ranch house. If Disney controls movement down Main Street, he also empowers the would-be actor to feel at home in an environment created precisely for that reason. Main Street is the home place that exists somewhere deep in the American psyche.

In a sense, the whole of Disneyland is a recapitulation of Main Street USA. In Frontierland, Main Street reappears as a cluster of board-fronted mercantiles, straight out of a Hopalong Cassidy movie. In Adventureland, it takes the form of a trading outpost, deep in a mysterious jungle clearing. In Fantasyland, it is a kind of neo-medieval mini-mart that opens from the rear of the castle, with bow windows and hints of thatch and turrets. The fundamen-tal transaction is one of interactive exchange. Dining. Shopping. American-style capitalism at a grassroots level, with which the guest in the exuberant retail environment of the 1950s (and the mall culture of the 21st century) was thoroughly at home. This

is the basis of museum culture, too. The museum-goer inspects artifacts—themed in this case—in order to learn and to enjoy. The twist is that in the stores of Main Street, you can take the exhibits home with you, after a chat with a clerk who looks like a frontier mother, a renegade member of a barbershop quartet, a too-large elf, or a grounded spaceman!

Main Street USA: welcome home, America! ◆

Fantasyland

4

FANTASYLAND

A world of the imagination, where the dreams of
childhood come true. Meet Snow White and the
Wicked Witch as you ride with the Seven Dwarfs
through their diamond mine. Fly with Peter Pan
over London-town to Never-Never Land. Board a
pirate ship. Visit Sleeping Beauty in her castle.
Join the Mad Hatter's Tea Party. Fly with Dumbo,
ride in Mr. Toad's auto or join the rollicking fun
on Casey Junior's Train . . . all these and many
more storybook characters wait to enchant you
in Fantasyland.

Spread from The Story of Disneyland, *1955*

At the very top of the heart-shaped footprint of Disneyland lies Fantasyland, in the controlling position—the consciousness, the imagination that dreamt the dream of this utopia. If Main Street USA came from Walt Disney's memory, then Fantasyland came straight from the particular genius that made him famous: the animated feature cartoon. This was the land of make-believe, storybooks, old fairytales made new for American children and their parents in the darkness of the local movie theater. Snow White. Alice in Wonderland. Peter Pan. Mr. Toad. Tea cups. Wicked stepmothers. Pirates. A beautiful carousel. The house of Pinocchio's long-suffering stepfather, Geppetto. And the spires of Sleeping Beauty Castle, in pinks and the softest of blues; the drawbridge over the moat led straight into a pastel haze of wonderment.

Walt Disney's empire was based on stories like these. Some were old, some newer, all filtered through the imagination of the man who acted out every episode for his animators, inspected every drawing and put his personal signature—the one he could no longer approximate in real life—on every remarkable movie, beginning with *Snow White and the Seven Dwarfs* in 1937. Like the later Disney classics, *Snow White* was a modern, made-for-Americans version of the Brothers Grimm narrative. Snow White is a down-to-earth child/woman who loves to keep house, scrubbing, cleaning and washing. She's sunny and friendly—to her peril, in the end, when the Evil Queen comes calling disguised as a warty old beggarwoman offering a poisoned apple.

But everything turns out fine. The dwarfs have their little mother back; the prince has his princess; the Queen gets her comeuppance. Nothing has been *too* scary along the way. The murderous woodsman turns out to be a nice fellow and the old crone with the apple is hideous enough to be almost funny, a sort of caricature of a true villainess. The moral aspects of the story and the sighs of contentment at the awakening of the heroine are secondary, nonetheless, to the visual delights of *Snow White*.

The most important of these is the rustic cottage of the dwarfs, nestled lovingly

in the peace of the forest. Here, the little princess finds refuge. Here, she toils with obvious pleasure. When she is separated from the pseudo-Germanic *gemutlichheit* of the cottage, that is when she falls into her deathlike sleep. After *Snow White* became a big box-office hit, the studio built a kid-size replica of that cottage for Walt's backyard. His two daughters seemed less interested in playing there than their father did. The triumph, the happiness and the plain Midwestern values represented by that cottage—that single movie frame brought to life—are the qualities that would inform Fantasyland almost two decades later.

Before defining exactly what wonders Disneyland would contain, Walt had sent out emissaries to famous amusement parks across the land. How did they handle crowds? What were the customary hours of operation? And, above all, what kept people coming back, season after season? His researchers spent little time on traditional roller coasters and the ancestors of today's thrill rides. The boss had something else in mind. But they could not have helped seeing one of the oldest amusement devices common to such resorts: the scenic boat ride through an interior space, often in near darkness.

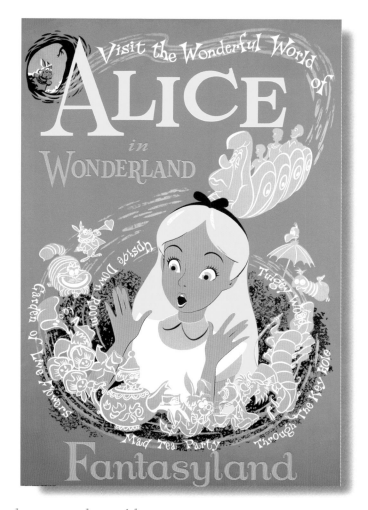

In some places, the trip was called "The Old Mill." Or "Creation." Or even "The Tunnel of Love." The original idea, dating back to the era of Main Street USA, was to present a series of scenic revelations as the boats glided by; in "Creation," for example Adam and Eve (in tights!) might be visible for an edifying second or two in a flash of illumination. But in the raucous Coney Islands of the early 20th century, boat rides proved ideal spots for surreptitious spooning. Hence "Tunnels of Love," of dubious reputation. One of Walt Disney's most important contributions to the annals of the outdoor amusement business was to retool and resuscitate what he called the "dark ride."

The most remarkable of the Park's early dark rides was based on Disney's version of *Peter Pan* (1953). Loosely adapted from the famous British play by James Barrie, the film described the adventures of the three Darling children, who fly off to Neverland in the company of a magical boychild and a temperamental sprite named Tinker Bell. The ride places the American family in a pirate ship, suspended in midair high above the city of London and finally over Neverland itself, swooping, circling, through the familiar intricacies of the story—all in a vast, dark space in which only the geography

Walt Disney revived the dark ride to create his most novel attractions. This drawing for the interior of an adventure based on the Disney version of Peter Pan *shows the elaborate settings through which little pirate ship ride vehicles, suspended from the ceiling, swoop and soar. The folks in the boats become the stars of the movie.*

below the ship is fitfully illuminated. The sensation of flight, the experience of soaring effortlessly into some strange and wondrous place, is disarming. But so is the implicit notion that the riders are characters in the movie. Against all reason, the family in the flying ship has navigated its way through the movie screen and into the heart of the action.

The guest is no mere observer in the Disneyland dark rides. He or she is a part of the drama, present in a convincing role. A similar attraction, based on *Snow White*, uses cars from the dwarfs' diamond mine to transport the guest into a dizzying sequence of brief, shocking moments of danger, capped off by the requisite happy ending. Until recently, Snow White was nowhere present in the ensemble. The person riding in the mine car filled in for the missing heroine and, in the process, became an integral element of the storyline. Or the star of the show.

The architectural style of Fantasyland, dictated by costs and the rush to complete the park before opening day, was inadvertently well suited to the notion of making every guest a movie star. Unlike Main Street USA, with its fully dimensional facades and finished interiors, the show buildings of Fantasyland were prefabricated industrial sheds, disguised in a colorful slipcover that suggested the fabric of tents set up for a medieval joust. The brainchild of Eyvind Earle, the same artist responsible for the flat, Cubist-influenced planes of *Sleeping Beauty*, the structures looked theatrical—like the elaborate stage curtains that whooshed back to reveal the screen in everybody's own home town movie palace. So the buildings of Fantasyland strengthened the sense of penetrating that flat screen, of walking however improbably, straight into a film in progress.

A cumulative series of what Walt called "plusses"—in 1959 and again in 1983—altered Fantasyland almost beyond recognition, by fronting several of the dark rides with Gothic and Tudor manor houses. But the real charm of the spot where Walt

One of the reasons that Disneyland was so delightful was the fact that every detail reinforced the narrative. This is a concept drawing for a toy store in Fantasyland, themed after Alice in Wonderland. *The grinning Cheshire Cat, borrowed directly from the Disney film, presides over the merchandise.*

*Early ideas for Fantasy-
land attractions, 1954:
King Arthur Carrousel
(above left); Casey Jr.
Circus Train (above right);
Storybook Land Canal
Boats (below left); Duck
Bumps (below right,
never built)*

Disney's animated features have come to life lies in the interiors, in the dark. Pictures published in *Life* magazine in 1955 showed a bleak, sun-baked Fantasyland, where the grass had failed to sprout and the trees had not yet begun to grow. The crowds are giddy with delight, however. They were taking part in a form of entertainment that was absolutely new and totally engaging when they lined up for "Peter Pan's Flight" or "Snow White's Scary Adventures." The on-site manager of Fantasyland, however, thought that the audience was bewildered by the lack of the central figure in the dark rides. As early as August of 1955, he was suggesting alterations (thirty years in the making) to add Snow White to her venue. But perhaps the problem he detected was bedazzlement

rather than confusion. In 1955, everything at Disneyland was new and different.

Legend has it that Walt tested out the effect of his innovative dark rides by crawling through a model of the scenery set up on a giant tabletop. Today's Disney Imagineers—the folks who build the parks—drag tiny "lipstick" cameras through models which can be assembled inside a cardboard box. The goal of the process remains the same. What will the rider see? What effect will the placement of a specific object have on the guest? The dark ride is constructed with the eye of a master director or cinematographer specifically to tell a story. On Main Street, the scenes through which the plot unfolds itself are determined block by block. In Fantasyland, they come

Early ideas for Fantasyland attractions, 1954: Peter Pan's Flight ride vehicle (above left); Snow White's Scary Adventures ride vehicle (above right); Dumbo the Flying Elephant (below left); Mad Tea Party (below right)

Where Dreams Really Do Come True

The castle is Disneyland's central landmark, its ultimate icon. It orients and guides guests—reassuring them that they are not lost, focusing their attention if they feel overwhelmed, beckoning them to what lies within and setting the mood for what lies beyond. It is the feature that, more than any other element, makes Disneyland magical.

Early on, Walt Disney had the idea that guests should enter Fantasyland through a fantastic castle. But what should this castle look like? Walt's Imagineers tried out plenty of ideas—from castles that were architecturally and historical accurate to those that drew from fantastic dreams and visions. In the end, they were most inspired by the picturesque towers and turrets of Neuschwanstein Castle in Bavaria. Still, Walt thought copying the actual castle was a little too realistic and was only satisfied when the top half of the real castle was turned around backwards. Taking their cue from a theatrical technique called forced perspective, Walt's designers then set about carving the stones in diminishing scale to make the building look taller than it really was.

The new castle was named after Sleeping Beauty—a pitch for Disney's new film-in-the-making. Beyond the walls of Sleeping Beauty Castle, guests enter "the happiest kingdom of them all"—Fantasyland. Sleeping Beauty Castle proved so successful in both the functions it served and its mood-setting appearance that castles became a standard central feature at all the Disney "Magic Kingdom" parks that followed.

Color concept for "Le Chateau de la Belle Au Bois Dormant"— the strikingly beautiful castle at Disneyland Paris (above right). Disneyland's Sleeping Beauty Castle in all its glory at night, in this early concept for lighting the Central Plaza during Christmas season, 1955 (right).

Guests spin madly inside tea cups at Fantasyland's Mad Tea Party, based upon Disney's Alice in Wonderland *animated film.*

thick and fast, with every separate attraction, from the people-size spinning tea cups to the carousel on which every single horse prances up and down as you ride.

Fantasyland, for all its novelty, is also a confectioner's recreation of the park as a whole, multiplying the impact of Disneyland in miniature. The Casey Jr. Circus Train is a case in point—a multi-colored, cartoonish version of the peripheral steam railroad line departing from the Main Street station. Casey was a three-dimensional copy of the train that appeared in the opening scenes of *Dumbo* (1941) and the little railroad was paired with a boat ride which, like the Park as a whole, added water features to the trackside scenery. The steam train whistles through Adventureland and Frontierland, passing by make-believe Amazon and Mississippi Rivers. Casey Jr., by the summer of 1956, passed through a miniature world containing the signature dwellings of the

*Herb Ryman's fantastically detailed rendering of
what Sleeping Beauty Castle might look like, 1954.
Walt showed this sketch to TV viewers (see page 27),
but the final castle ended up looking somewhat less
realistic and more make-believe.*

© 1963 BY
WED ENTERPRISES, INC.

Mary Blair's combination of unique, mood-setting backgrounds and cute-as-a-button figures delighted guests to "it's a small world" at the 1964 New York World's Fair.

beloved heroes and heroines of the animated features, including Snow White, Cinderella, and the rest, sited in a landscape composed of artfully stunted plants and microscopic gardens. "Storybook Land," as this precinct of Fantasyland was called, included the train, the rivers, a little castle and an assortment of references to previous Disney projects. In effect, it replicated Disneyland in Fantasyland in a new vocabulary of utterly familiar symbols.

There is a purposefulness in the decision to repeat the Park in each of its constituent parts. There are Main Streets in Frontierland, Adventureland and Tomorrowland, dressed up in period costume. And castles of a sort, too, in the form of the design elements Walt called "wienies"—attractive destinations for the eye which both articulated the space and made walking somehow easier and more pleasurable. It is as if Walt Disney had hit upon a configuration of sights and memories, places and imaginings

Just as the style of Disney's films changed, so did the look of Disneyland. When "it's a small world," originally developed for the 1964 New York World's Fair, opened at Disneyland, the re-designed facade brought a touch of abstraction to the park. This section describes Europe, with simplified versions of the Leaning Tower of Pisa and the Cathedral of Notre Dame.

that made an American, circa 1955, feel wholly delighted and content. Even if that hypothetical American hated waiting in line.

One of the best features of the dark rides, from the managerial point of view, was that they acted as people-pumps: the flow of riders on and off the vehicles was both continuous and endless, reducing wait time and maximizing the efficiency of the operation. Like an assembly line for merrymakers, the system added modern American know-how to old-fashioned ways of doing things. The people-pump concept reached a new height of sophistication with the "it's a small world" attraction, brought back from the New York World's Fair of 1964; here, loading and leaving the boats

Stylist Mary Blair discusses the design for "it's a small world" with Walt Disney.

Fantasyland   63

occurred simultaneously, increasing the number of riders handled in a given period of time exponentially. In other words, Disneyland "plussed" the art of crowd movement in a distinctively contemporary way, suited to a world of perpetual motion, swelling population figures and greater leisure time in which to enjoy Walt Disney's new Park.

The repetitive configuration of retail streetscape, railroad and historical trappings has little to do with efficiency but everything to do with the red-white-and-blue American-ness of Disneyland. Created in the boom years of the postwar era, the restatement of the primary planning unit suggests a continuity between past and future, with the visitor supplying the present tense. Fantasyland, Frontierland, Tomorrowland: they are essentially the same places. The notion is reassuring. Full of excitement and discovery, tomorrows are nothing to be feared. The past is still with us, purged of its flaws and imperfections. The dreams of childhood really can come true. Old and young, retrospection and vision, once upon a time and times yet to come are thoroughly mixed together into a spiritual concoction that is as meaningful today as it was in July of 1955. The very structure of Disneyland exudes the all-American, Midwestern optimism basic to the psyche of its creator. Fantasyland lays out his accomplishments as the nation's storyteller, our designated dreamer, the man who understood best the reveries of the eager child in all of us. ✦

The Fantasyland that Walt Really Wanted

Walt had envisioned Fantasyland as a quaint fairy-tale village. But the budget was tight as Opening Day drew near so many of the attractions there went through what we politely call today "value engineering." Buildings for the dark rides became flat-fronted, prefabricated industrial sheds decorated with pennants and ribbons to resemble tents at a medieval jousting tournament (right, above). Interior details for the rides were stylized, with a linear, sketchy quality. And that's the way they remained for more than 25 years.

In the early 1980s, Disney Imagineers decided to give Fantasyland a major facelift, to resolve the multiple problems of aging shows, a land that was looking outdated and major congestion inside the Castle courtyard. Although they were nervous about virtually undoing a land that Walt himself had had such a close hand in creating, they drew inspiration from a charming little attraction that had opened way back in 1956 and was still going strong—the Storybook Land Canal Boats (right, middle). Here guests ride on boats past exquisite miniature vignettes from Walt's classic animated films. Imagineers believed that along the shores of this boat ride were the templates for the quaint homes and villages that Walt would have created in Fantasyland if the money hadn't run out. So they set about redesigning and rearranging many of the attractions, and even added a few new ones.

The new Fantasyland, which opened in 1983, is charming, whimsical and richly three-dimensional (right, below). Many guests probably believe this is the original Fantasyland. And that's just how it should be!

5
Frontierland

FRONTIERLAND

Enter through the massive log gates of an old 18th century fort into the world of yesterday. Ride in a buckboard, a Conestoga wagon, a Concord stage, or even on a pack mule train to the colorful Painted Desert. Cruise the rivers of America, past historic landmarks and colorful river towns, on a 105-foot paddle wheel boat.

Our country's exciting past is accurately reproduced in Frontierland.

Tinker Bell, in a feathered headband, does a comic war dance. Drumbeats. The voice-over—a silky male voice—announces "…tall tales and true from the legendary past." October 27, 1954. The new *Disneyland* show is on the air. And this is the logo for "Frontierland," one of the four Wednesday-night themes the home audience might enjoy that week. Under this title, in mid-December, the program presented the first in a series of made-for-TV adventures of the coonskin Congressman and yarn-spinner, Davy Crockett. Walt Disney faced the camera, holding a big, leather-bound book entitled, "Davy Crockett's Journal." And one of the great national crazes of the 1950s began.

Spread from The Story of Disneyland, 1955

First, came the theme song: "Born on a mountaintop in Tennessee… kilt him a bar, when he was only three." Davy Crockett, King of the Wild Frontier! By Thursday afternoon, half of the nation's schoolchildren were humming the catchy tune, attempting to hypnotize the family cat by grinning at it (the Crockett method for subduing bears, a.k.a. "bars"), and wondering when the next part of the story would emerge. They didn't have long to wait. In January, 1955, the erstwhile Indian fighter was elected to Congress and, in February, he went down in glory defending

Walt shares a moment with Fess Parker on the Davy Crockett set.

the Alamo against the army of Mexican General Santa Anna.

Later in 1955, with Fess Parker (Davy) and his sidekick, Buddy Ebsen (George Russel) overnight stars, the three episodes were edited together into a movie. Lines stretched around the block everywhere. In numbers unseen since the raccoon coat craze of the 1920s, fur-bearing animals were sacrificed on the altar of juvenile fashion: pity the child whose parents could not provide Junior and Sis with authentic as-seen-on-TV Davy Crockett coonskin caps! Or, at the very least, a T-shirt, or a plastic powderhorn. A rubber Bowie knife.

Whatever and whoever the real David Crockett may have been, the Disney version treated his highly embellished adventures in a serio-comic manner. Parker's Davy brags, blusters and performs miraculous feats of derring-do at every turn, reminding the grownups that he was the spiritual father of Buffalo Bill, William S. Hart and the Lone Ranger—of every tall-tale, rootin'-tootin' hero spawned by the epic of the American frontier. Pulp fiction, to be sure, coexisted with serious novels of the West, such as Owen Wister's *The Virginian* (1902), dedicated to Theodore Roosevelt, a leading expo-nent of a "strenuous" outdoor life in an era of increasing urbanization.

The theme proved particularly germane to readers in the years after World War II. Louis L'Amour, a former tank officer, found his civilian calling as the author of a string of bestsellers based on the strength and endurance of the men who won the West. In the process, he virtually reinvented paperback adventure literature for returning

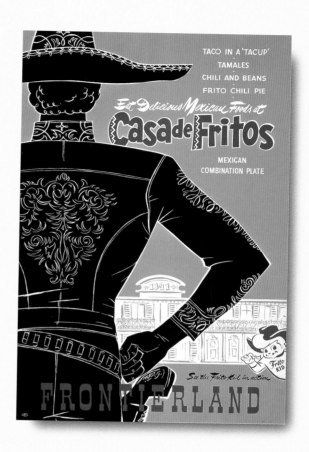

veterans like himself—and spawned the scripts for more than thirty popular films. At the end of the 1940s and the beginning of the '50s, John Ford began his celebrated Cavalry Trilogy, *Red River* made John Wayne the quintessential cowboy star, and careers of aging Western actors—Roy Rogers and Hopalong Cassidy—were given new life on afternoon TV shows for children made up of excerpts from their old B films. Riding the range and grinning down "bars" were both part of the fabric of American life in the 1950s.

The Davy Crockett fad and the Frontierland attractions at Disneyland answered real cultural needs. Suburbanites lived in ranch-style houses, as young families abandoned crowded city streets for the endless lawns—the plains—of the subdivision. In a sense, these were the pioneers of a new frontier and a new lifestyle, predicated on male prowess in the workplace. If Moms were to stay home, as the magazine ads showing happy housewives strongly suggested, then Dads had to kill the metaphorical "bars" for the stewpot (or the neighborhood barbecue) even if work increasingly meant a 9-to-5

Walt showed this evocative charcoal rendering on TV to describe Frontierland. A view from the Hub in front of the Castle, the picture shows the fort that marks the gateway, a frontier town beyond it and the Mark Twain riverboat. But it is also dramatic and exciting, with its tepees, Indians, schoolmarms, cowboys and cavalrymen, all in motion.

office grind on the corporate treadmill. The open spaces of the suburbs offered compensation for the confinement of suit and tie. After hours, men adopted the do-it-yourself movement in order to regain a sense of instrumentality (or add a carport to the house): they *could* make something tangible with their own two hands! As head of a growing corporation, Walt Disney himself experienced many of the same frustrations—and dealt with them by building his miniature railroads and dreaming his oversize dreams. He understood the dilemma of the 1950s and addressed it directly in Disneyland's Frontierland.

The attractions of Frontierland, in keeping with the historical "feel" of 19th-century America, were less spectacular and certainly less technologically sophisticated than the dark rides of Fantasyland. On opening day, the biggest draw was the Mississippi riverboat, the steam-driven paddlewheeler christened the "Mark Twain." With its tall stacks and earsplitting whistle, the boat amounted to the "wienie" for Frontierland, the symbolic core of the place, visible (or audible) from the Hub. The trip down the generic "Rivers of America" took the passengers past an Indian village, populated in the summer

This is a second calmer and more analytical version of the same "scene" by Herbert Ryman. Multiple studies of every detail show the painstaking way in which Walt Disney aimed to enhance the illusions of Disneyland.

Mark Twain, Another Missouri Boy

In the early plans for Frontierland, Walt was definite about wanting an old-time riverboat that would paddle down a river and around an island. He wanted guests on this riverboat to "take a scenic journey down the Rivers of America." But no one knew quite what to do with the island. Ideas like Mickey Mouse Island, Treasure Island and a display of miniature replicas of famous American landmarks along the edges of the island were brought up and discarded. Just before Disneyland opened, however, Walt's Imagineers realized that drawing upon the mythology created by author Mark Twain was the perfect solution to their dilemma.

Samuel Clemens grew up in Missouri, just like Walt, and they shared similar Midwestern values. He had grown up along the Missouri River, and much of his writing was oriented around river life. In fact his pen name Mark Twain was an old boatman's cry that meant the ship had found the deep center of the river. And, happily, he had already created an entire world of stories and characters based around the river and riverboat culture.

Before long, the 5/8-scale, steam-powered paddle-wheeler (the first one built in America in 50 years) was named the "Mark Twain Riverboat." Next, the Imagineers got busy and came up with plenty of adventures on the newly named Tom Sawyer Island. Log "rafts" (powered by diesel engines) ferried guests to the island, which came to include such elements from Mark Twain's stories as Injun Joe's Cave (where you could discover hidden treasure), the Old Mill (with its rotating waterwheel), and a suspension bridge across which you could carefully wend your way. For a time, guests could even fish off the Fishing Pier there. Mark Twain himself would have probably gotten a good chuckle out of the whole thing.

These early concepts reinforced the theme of Mark Twain's stories on paper, setting the mood and adventurous tone for the Island right from the start (above and left).

of 1955 by Native American dancers, and past a perpetually burning cabin, in front of which lay a dead settler with an arrow in his back. It was a simple ride through what passed for historical scenery. The only bells and whistles were those aboard the steamboat.

Over time, in response to changing perceptions about white America's violent seizure of the West, however, the burning cabin became a prime example of a careless settler menacing the ecology of the wilderness. Live Native Americans vanished, replaced by robotic versions. Today, a peaceful brave powered by wires and puffs of air solemnly greets each riverboat as it steams along. The changes illustrate gradual and sometimes overlooked alterations in Disneyland made to accommodate contemporary readings of history and the sensibilities of a multi-racial society. Well into the 20th century, fairs and expositions had routinely exhibited Native Americans and peoples of all kinds and colors in "villages" meant to be educational—or, if not educational, at least exotic and profitable. North American tribesmen, Africans and Asians all took their turns in quasi-anthropological displays in which the subjects dwelt and worked for the duration of the event, rather like captive animals in zoos. This kind of casual racism was still the order of the day in the 1950s, when the Civil Rights Movement had not yet gathered strength and suburbia took it as a given that persons of color dare not live in their neighborhood.

On the other hand, Mexican culture—and especially Mexican food—was given a prominence that must have been suprising to tourists from other parts of the country.

A shooting gallery built into the side of the fort is brought to life by the presence of a cowboy in full regalia.

As a horseman and a Californian, Disney had great respect for the old, landed families of his adopted state and their way of life. In addition, in 1955 he was already involved in the production of a new TV series based on the fictional doings of Zorro, the masked avenger of Spanish California. *Zorro* made its debut in 1957 and promptly touched off another frenzy of buying. This time, the desired items included black capes and masks, lariats, signet rings and almost anything adorned with the hero's trademark "Z." A second mini-series, entitled *The Nine Lives of Elfago Baca*, took for its hero a reformed Latino gunfighter from New Mexico, whose rip-snorting autobiography was published in 1944. So, while parts of Frontierland smack of Hollywood simplifications—good guys vs. bad guys, hostile "Injun" foes, knight-errant cowboys jousting for the honor of calico princesses—other elements in the mix introduce a taste of the colorful, touristic Old Mexico unique to California and the Southwest.

Many of the original diversions of Frontierland proved to be short-lived. A horse-drawn stagecoach line disappeared in 1960, a victim of low capacity and high costs, when the tendency of the vehicles to tip over and injure passengers was factored into the equation. The same fate befell the park's Conestoga wagons. A pack-mule ride through artificial rock work, added to Frontierland in 1957 to give visitors more to do there, also faded into oblivion over time. Animal rides were unpredictable and increasingly perceived as cruel. And they were by no means unique to Disneyland: small Western parks scattered from

An interior view of the Golden Horseshoe Saloon juxtaposes modern couples with Old West desperadoes (opposite).

Young guests cross over the Natural Bridge during their 10-minute mule pack ride in Frontierland (below).

Knott's Berry Farm to upstate New York's Frontiertown specialized in this kind of entertainment. Shouldn't Disneyland offer something bigger and better? One of the many ironies of Frontierland in 1955 was the fact that as the myth of the West gained ground

in popular entertainment and literature, its real-life discomforts and dangers became less and less attractive to a nation accustomed to going West in two-tone tail-fin cars. And that, at the moment when the Western saga exerted its most powerful influence on American life, it should also have come into question as a sugarcoated national falsehood.

Nonetheless, Frontierland provides the clearest connection between Hollywood movie sets and the intended effect of Disneyland. One of the principal buildings of Frontierland in 1955 was the Golden Horseshoe Saloon—strictly soft drinks and five family shows a day. When the scenic artist working on the project asked Walt to describe what he wanted for the saloon, Disney asked for something like the barroom in *Calamity Jane* (1953), the popular Doris Day musical Western. As it turned out, the artist Walt sent to research that movie was the man who designed the original set for Warner Brothers in the first place. He simply rebuilt the Doris Day scenery at a reduced scale. The Frontierland saloon is, in every particular, a movie set, with the typical American family cast as extras.

When Disneyland was replicated and adapted to other locations—Florida (1971),

Westward Ho!

Frontierland in the early days was full of rides—real rides inspired by the mythology of self-reliant mountain men and intrepid pioneers. For example, brave "mule skinners" could take a 10-minute mule pack ride over Frontierland's western landscape (including a "Natural Bridge"). Unfortunately, like real life, the mules were unpredictable—they might bolt quickly, stop and refuse to move, nibble on a guest's hat or hair, or bray loudly and cantankerously. Other frontier explorers could take their chances on a stagecoach—either riding "shotgun" atop the coach or sitting in relative safety but all cramped up inside. Once again, catastrophe was just around the corner. The stagecoach was known to tip over; once the horses even got away!

But here at last was a ride that seemed to be without mishap. The Reel-Ride was all about your imagination. The horses were mechanical. The adventure was on screen. You even got to become part of the movies and ride with a real movie star. We'll probably never know why this ride never came to be.

A "Reel-Ride" with a favorite cowboy star - as he chases and captures a villian.

children mounted on mechanical horses which are synchronized with a back-projection on a translucent screen, giving effect of actually travelling through the country. When chase is ended - horses stop.

Rides will last 3 to 5 minutes.

Grim Grinning Ghosts

Well? Are they grim or are they grinning? This question "haunted" Disney's Imagineers for years as they sketched out idea after idea for the Haunted Mansion. It started in 1951, with Harper Goff's sketch of an eerie haunted house at the edge of a small-town Main Street. By the late 1950s, the mansion had been relocated to New Orleans Square—a new land that would transition between Adventureland and Frontierland. The loose concept was that it would be a "retirement home for all the world's restless spirits." But what would the mansion look like? And what was the guest experience? Neither of these questions was easy to solve, it turned out.

Walt rejected every early sketch in which the mansion or its grounds looked neglected or decaying. He declared that the exterior should look clean and attractive—like the rest of the architecture at New Orleans Square and in keeping with what guests expected at Disneyland. The house was finally constructed in 1963, but it lay empty inside as the project was put on hold for the New York World's Fair. The "haunting"—whatever that was to be—would just have to wait.

Unfortunately, Walt didn't live long enough to see this attraction completed. Meanwhile, Imagineers argued about whether it should be ominous and scary or upbeat and funny. The final attraction, which opened in 1969, ended up a combination of these. Illusions, special effects, atmospheric backgrounds and entertaining characters are plentiful—all pulled together by an upbeat song and a disembodied "Ghost Host" whose voice is piped into guests' "doom buggies."

The anticipation for this attraction was so great that one week after opening it set a record for attendance in one day (82,516 guests)! This record went unbroken in the Park for more than 15 years.

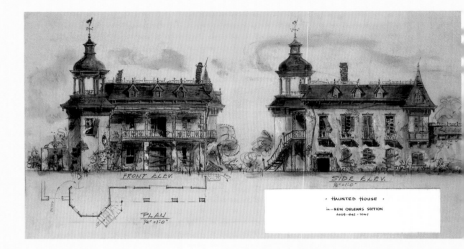

Walt Disney rejected early concepts of spooky and ramshackle haunted mansions, as not appropriate to what guests would expect at Disneyland.

Tokyo (1983), Paris (1992)—Frontierland underwent a variety of changes, none more extensive than in France, where the cult of the mythic Old West was countered by a strong interest in Native American history and artifacts. The Paris version of Frontierland includes a ranch, a tumbledown ghost-town version of the Haunted Mansion and archaeologically precise presentations of Indian culture. The trick has been to retain the romance of freedom, self-reliance and expansiveness while acknowledging other, less savory realities. And it is important to recognize that for practical, economic and ideological reasons, the Disney parks—and Walt Disney's Frontierland—will always be in flux, like the American frontier itself.

"Disneyland is your land," reads the dedicatory plaque, repeating Walt's speech of welcome. "Here age relives fond memories of the past." But memories fade and change, like the dreams and the nightmares that commingle in the smoke of a burning log cabin. ✦

Only the top portions of these paintings are revealed when guests first step into the "dead center" of the Haunted Mansion's Stretching Room. But, when the entrance disappears and the lights go out, the walls and paintings seem to "stretch," revealing the comically creepy fate of each figure.

6 Adventureland

ADVENTURELAND

"The wonderland of Nature's own design," Walt Disney
Here you can stroll through a Tahitian village lush in i
beauty, marvel at the unusual exhibit of South Seas
displayed at the Bazaar, or take an explorer's boat on a
through tropical rivers where life-like wild animals add th
excitement to your trip to the far ends of the world.

Spread from The Story of Disneyland, *1955*

ain Street divides Disneyland roughly in two. On the right side—the east side, on most maps—lies Tomorrowland, the future, a world of concrete and electronics. The left or western half of the park contains, by contrast, the natural world: the forests and plains of Frontierland; the jungles and tropical isles of Adventureland. In the east, the sun rises over tomorrow. In the west, it sets over a natural landscape, ripe for the plundering. To paraphrase the title of one of Disney's great documentaries of the 1950s, Adventureland was part of *A Vanishing Wilderness*.

The documentary in question, *The Vanishing Prairie*, was released in 1954, the second in a series of feature-length films called the "True-Life Adventures." These combined remarkable nature footage with majestic scores often synchronized to the movements of the animals and narration sometimes criticized for explaining animal behavior in all-too-human terms. Whatever their failings, the "True-Life" films and the related "People and Places" shorts, begun in 1953, were a departure from the usual studio fare, part old-fashioned travelogue and part a foretaste of *Nature* and the *Discovery Channel* yet to come. The popularity of the "True-Life" series in the early 1950s, as the first crop of memoirs and novels about the GI's encounter with far-off places began to appear, points to an emerging sense that the world was bigger than Iowa or upstate New York. And most of that world still belonged to Mother Nature, despite the incursions of human warfare and the exploitation of natural resources.

The Broadway musical, *South Pacific* (1949), based on James Michener's stories of military duty in an exotic setting, set the tone for a spate of Hollywood movies of the 1950s: *Mogambo* (1953), *Elephant Walk* (1954), *Bwana Devil* (1953; the first 3-D movie) and one of Walt Disney's personal favorites, *The African Queen* of 1951. In *The African Queen*, Katharine Hepburn and Humphrey Bogart sail a rattletrap boat through the African jungles during World War I as wild animals (represented in stock footage) menace their

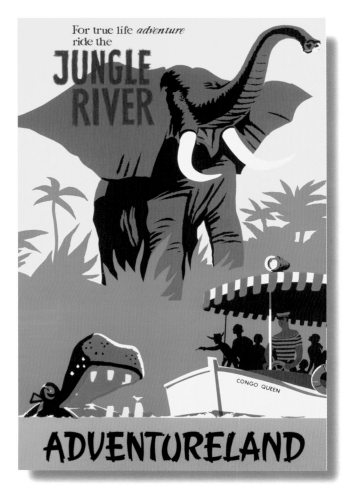

craft from shore. This was the boat and the scenario Disney chose for his Jungle Cruise, the "E" ticket attraction in Adventureland (so-called for the most exciting rides and thus most expensive tickets in guests' admission booklets) —and the park's most popular ride for the remainder of the 1950s.

This adventure was by no means easy to recreate. There was a river to build (twin to the "Rivers of America" in nearby Frontierland). A jungle to simulate through the magic of imaginative horticulture. And wild animals. From zookeepers and park owners, Walt soon learned about the hazards of using live creatures that slept during daylight hours and were disinclined to appear on cue every time a boat passed by. Instead, Disney and his colleagues designed mechanical animals: ferocious hippos and elephants and crocodiles which menaced each and every batch of jungle adventurers in just the same way and obediently slithered away on command from the fearless guide who piloted each craft. That these were not live animals and that the audience seemed to like the plastic substitutes better bothered some critics, although the average American family at Disneyland for the day showed little desire to take up extreme tourism on the Congo or the Amazon. Indeed, the pleasure of the ride came from being Bogart or Hepburn, matrixed in the make-believe of a movie. A real hippo was serious business. A Disney hippo was fun, safe and a goad to the imagination.

Walt Disney had experimented with robotics earlier, before the park was built, when, as a hobbyist, he made miniature scenes populated by balky moving figures. But the Jungle Cruise was his first venture into a wholesale involvement in the technology of three-dimensional animation triggered by recorded sound, or what he later called Audio-Animatronics®. Such devices were the cornerstone of Disney's efforts to "plus" the Park in the decade after the gala opening, in answer to complaints that there wasn't enough to see and do at Disneyland. And Disney himself wanted to open new themed restaurants to enhance the sensual experience of the various "lands." In Adventureland, the plussing began with the Enchanted Tiki Room, originally planned as a Stouffer's restaurant, offering the popular Hawaiian/Pacific cuisine that was sweeping the country. But the finest minds on his staff failed to come up with a way to entertain the diners and still persuade them to clear out after one hour, so the next sitting could begin.

Walt soon learned about the hazards of using live creatures that slept during daylight hours and were disinclined to appear on cue every time a boat passed by.

In the end, the tables and the Pupu platters disappeared and the decorations—stuffed birds in the rafters, artificial flowers, "native" carvings on the walls—became actors in a sparkling electronic performance. The Enchanted Tiki Room opened as a show in June, 1963. During an episode of his new, full-color NBC weekly TV show, Walt personally introduced this "new medium," in the person of a little toucan with brass innards, a feather overcoat, and the ability to perform a series of simple movements while chirping in time with the rest of the flock. A similar bird would perch on Julie Andrews' finger during a musical number from *Mary Poppins* (1964), but the most lasting impact of the technology came in the family of Disney theme parks.

The boats—and the idea for Jungle Cruise—came from a non-Disney movie, The African Queen, *starring Humphrey Bogart and Katharine Hepburn.*

On October 31, 1966, two months before Walt's death, engineers flooded another river and tried out a dark ride wholly premised on robotic pirates pillaging the Caribbean. Although the attraction was officially located in the new New Orleans Square, adjacent to Adventureland, the jolly pirate crew was a sophisticated extension of the themes and the technology of the old Jungle Cruise. The press hailed

*Colorful poster composition
for Adventureland's Tahitian
Terrace, about 1962*

Aloha!

In the early 1960s, Americans went head over heels for Pacific Island culture. A new fondness for all things Polynesian was spurred on by Hawaii's statehood, the popularity of Thor Heyerdahl's book *Kon-Tiki*, and a spate of popular movies (including *South Pacific* in 1958 and Elvis Presley's *Blue Hawaii* in 1961). Tiki restaurants cropped up in every city, Tahiti became a favored vacation destination for the jet set, and backyard luaus were staged by suburban trendsetters.

A Polynesian-themed food experience seemed destined for Adventureland. The Tahitian Terrace, open in 1962, seemed to do the trick. It featured a Hawaiian-themed interior, exotic dancing and live shows out on the terrace in the summer, along with exotic-sounding dishes like Wa'hi Maha'na Hou Hua Salada ("a bouquet of tropical fruit with lime sherbet on shredded lettuce").

Meanwhile Walt and his staff were busily working on an even more ambitious restaurant concept—an "Enchanted Tiki Room" (top, right). But the show concept soon became so long and complex that the restaurant was eliminated and the attraction was born instead.

Today, the Tahitian Terrace is long gone (vestiges of it live on at the Polynesian Resort at Walt Disney World in Florida), and the Enchanted Tiki Room has been upgraded to better match the attention span of modern audiences. But interest in Polynesian culture lives on, and who knows? A full-blown Tiki revival could be just around the corner.

Souvenir salt and pepper shakers, 1960s.

The dramatic Adventureland entrance immediately puts guests in the mood for their adventure ahead.

Pirates of the Caribbean as a "space-age" marvel. Nobody lamented the absence of live pirates. And the ride remains a masterpiece of all-encompassing, environmental showmanship.

There is a strange connection between technology and the Third World atmosphere of Adventureland. A massive artificial tree made of steel and concrete appeared there in 1962. Capable of supporting the weight of as many tourists as wished to climb its branches into the treehouse of the "Swiss Family Robinson" (the theme of a new Disney live-action movie; today, it's Tarzan's house, named for a recent animated feature), the tree outdid nature, with more of that space-age know-how. The buildings containing the shops and snack stations of Adventureland also acknowledge the incursions of Western technology into the realm of nature. The structures are patched with corrugated iron sheets and decorated with scroll-cut gingerbread trim. If this once was the utopian, unspoiled paradise of the imagination, it is now a distant colony of Anaheim, California.

One of the latest additions to Adventureland, completed in 1995, alludes to Walt Disney's admiration for the work of other filmmakers. In 1955, John Huston's *African Queen* had been the template for the Jungle Cruise. Forty years later, the movieland hero of the day was the swashbuckling archaeologist brought to life by George Lucas in his adventure-packed *Indiana Jones* films. So "Indy," or an Audio-Animatronics® version of Harrison Ford, joined the cast of Adventureland in a dark ride that energized the genteel exoticism of the 1950s with a walloping dose of contemporary special effects, as the ride vehicle lurches, jerks, reverses direction and tears along through a tapestry of snakes and rats and other vile obstacles in the rider's path toward untold riches hidden in the Temple of the Forbidden Eye. The Huston film maintained a certain decorum, on which the story hinged. The Lucas film aimed at the spills and thrills once associated with roller coasters.

Adventureland offers both versions, with the delights of perpetually singing artificial birds thrown in for good measure and a crew of unscary pirates just around the corner. It is a retro, space-age adventure straight out of the sensibilities of the 1950s, spiced with new fables for those of us whose biggest adventure is apt to be a trip to Disneyland. ✦

The longest lines in today's Disneyland are often for a ride based on the popular Indiana Jones *films, by George Lucas. This 1992 sketch describes the tottering rocks, the burning torches, the buried temples—and Jones himself, seen by riders in the form of an advanced version of the plastic hippos of 1955.*

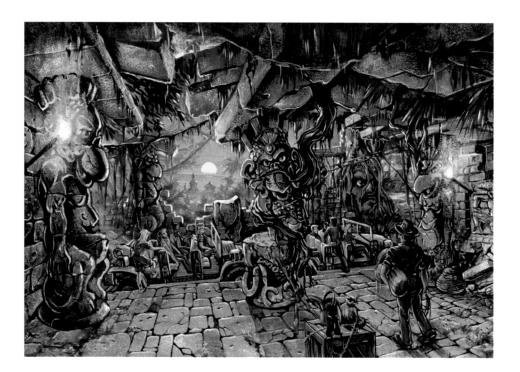

A Pirate's Life for Me

Walt had always wanted "some kind of pirate attraction" in the Park. For years, his Imagineers toyed with various ideas, including an underground Pirate Wax Museum. Among the creative concept designers was animator Marc Davis, who was known for developing characters that added humor and irony to various attractions. At first, Marc researched real pirates, but he soon discovered that their stories weren't very family-friendly. So he and others worked to "lighten up" the sequence of scenes that would portray the exploits of the "wildest crew that ever sacked the Spanish Main." Finally, after hundreds of sketches, the development of more advanced Audio-Animatronics® technology, the invention of new water ride-through vehicles, and a rousing pirate song, "Pirates of the Caribbean" was born.

This thrilling adventure begins as guests board "bateaux"—flat-bottomed boats used in the Louisiana swamps (right, below). They slowly leave the safety of the Louisiana bayou and journey deep into the Caribbean. The bateaux splash down a waterfall right into an eerie cavern, where guests hear a disembodied voice ominously warning them, "Dead men tell no tales." Then it's on to Dead Man's Cove, through the midst of a battle between a pirate ship and a fortress (cannon balls whistle a few inches overhead), and past the streets of a full-scale Caribbean port which is under attack by pirates. Chaos and bedlam are the order of the day, in an exciting but tongue-in-cheek sort of way.

The ride lasts 15 minutes. When it's over, it's hard for guests to believe that they were really in sunny California all along. This guest favorite, opened in New Orleans Square in 1967, provided the inspiration for the highly popular movie of 2003.

1965 concepts for the dungeon scene and Caribbean port under attack.

Tomorrowland

7

TOMORROWLAND

Here you find the future in the present as you ride a r
to the moon or board a space ship at the Space Port. I
two exciting exhibit buildings packed with architectura
industrial displays, you can see and experience today
tomorrow's living will be like by operating the push-b
controls.

Whatever your dreams of the future may be, you
find them all realized in Tomorrowland.

In Walt Disney's own mind, there were strong connections between his True-Life adventure films and the world of the future. In an early memo describing his intentions for a three-part *Disneyland* series called "Man in Space," he suggested that the new shows, like the nature episodes, would succeed only if they present-

Spread from The Story of Disneyland, *1955*

ed serious ideas in an entertaining manner. If Frontierland and "Davy Crockett" mixed history and tall tales to paint a compelling vision of the past, then Tomorrowland and "Man in Space" could look forward by combining hard science and science fiction fantasy. In fact, sci-fi was among the most popular imaginative themes of the 1950s. Kids thrilled to *Tom Corbett: Space Cadet* on Saturday morning TV, while the Disney Studios would soon contribute special effects expertise to *Forbidden Planet* (released in 1956), a CinemaScope space-age version of Shakespeare's *The Tempest*— starring Robby the Robot. In the wake of World War II, with a consumer boom and a nuclear threat both high on the national agenda, the future loomed ever closer. Walt Disney would have a major role to play in telling America what its real-life Tomorrowland might look like.

The first segment of "Man in Space" aired repeatedly in 1955 and 1956, by popular demand. President Eisenhower requested a copy of the show to screen for the rocket

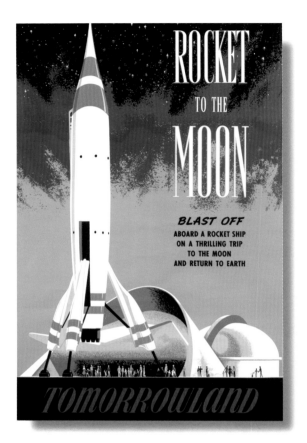

experts at the Pentagon. Indeed, it seems likely that many of Eisenhower's policy decisions about the space race (including an announcement that the United States would put a satellite into orbit during the 1957 International Geophysical Year) arose from public demand for action triggered by "Man in Space," with its cast of famous scientists, including the mesmerizing Wernher von Braun, once Germany's foremost rocket scientist. When von Braun described the journey to Mars as if astronauts might leave under nuclear power at any moment, the "Rocket to the Moon" attraction at Disneyland, introduced by a towering space ship bearing the airline logo of TWA, seemed both plausible and thrilling.

On Opening Day, Danny Thomas described the rocket ride to the television audience: the space passengers seated in tiers of special protective chairs; the roar and the vibration as the launch vehicle cleared the earth; the planet growing smaller in the lower viewing port while the stars and planets came closer and closer in the ceiling port. It was convincing and amazing. Surely TWA, American Airlines and United Airlines would be selling tickets to Mars within the lifetimes of today's Disneyland pioneers! Tomorrowland was "set" in 1986 (the year in which Halley's Comet would reappear)—so the wonders of the space age were just around the corner.

Unfortunately, they were not quite ready for 1955, however. The first public countdown to moon launch was delayed until July 22 because Tomorrowland was not quite finished. In the fall of 1954, with funds running low, subordinates urged Walt to admit that this quadrant of the park would never be ready in time. Better to scuttle Tomorrowland for now. Yet Disney refused to do so. The first nuclear power plant had just opened. It didn't take a rocket scientist to discern that a technological revolution was in full swing in the laboratories and in the nation's new shopping malls. Disneyland needed what Walt called "the daring land of dreams and hopes upon which the future rests."

Tomorrowland opened on schedule, although most of the space was taken up by balloons that masked a dearth of futuristic things to do. The most visible attraction was a display made up of sets and props from 20,000 *Leagues Under the Sea* (1954), Disney's first theatrical venture into science fiction, which is a kind of retrospective view of tomorrow as seen by Jules Verne and his hero, Captain Nemo, commander of a Victorian submarine complete with an ornate pipe organ. This was the future, 19th-century style. As for the rest, Tomorrowland for many years served as a kind of permanent trade fair, with space for rent in which corporations could set up their own displays of modern merchandise with today's consumer in mind. There were new cars, a Crane Bathroom of Tomorrow (created by noted industrial designer Henry Dreyfuss), a Dairy of the Future, a Color Gallery displaying Dutch Boy brand paints, and a Richfield Oil diorama of gas-guzzling Southern California.

The best thing in Tomorrowland, in the opinion of young

Who's the Spaceman Now?

Back in the early 1960s, reported sightings of UFO's (Unidentified Flying Objects) were a common occurrence. Many people took seriously the possibility that curious life forms from other planets were actually interested in checking out Earth and its inhabitants. So it seemed only natural that Disneyland should have a Flying Saucer attraction in Tomorrowland. From 1961 to 1966, guests could board these "bumper cars of the future" in the hopes of plowing into as many other saucers as possible before their time was up.

The saucers were actually lifted up a few inches off the floor by bursts of air blasted from below ground. Alas, the flying saucers caused no end of problems: heavy people wouldn't move anywhere, lighter people bounced up and down, saucers careened crazily across the arena as people shifted their weight, a speeding saucer might even flip another saucer over if the two collided just right! It's amazing, in retrospect, that the Flying Saucers lasted five whole years.

Guests "fly" through "space" on their Flying Saucers, while others look on in amusement.

FLY YOUR OWN **FLYING SAUCER**

space terminal in *TOMORROWLAND*

Californians, was the Autopia. Elsewhere in Disneyland, and especially in later versions of Tomorrowland, Walt continued to challenge the primacy of the automobile in the U.S. transportation network. His monorail system, dedicated in 1959, his Viewliner train, and his experimental People Mover systems all aimed to lure Americans back to efficient public transit by example. But the little fiberglass cars zooming around a freeway of the very near future proved irresistible. On Opening Day, there were 35 cars ready to go. By closing time, with lines stretching to infinity under a blazing sun and equipment broken down all along the right of way, prospective motorists were pulling people out of the cars for their chance behind the wheel. This one concession to real life, circa 1955, overshadowed everything else—and accurately predicted the future of California.

The business of predicting was not always that easy. If Disney's Imagineers got it right in their Tomorrowland displays, then things looked old-fashioned almost overnight: the future caught up with hypothetical tomorrows with amazing speed.

Walt wanted Autopia to teach kids safe driving on the country's new freeways. Here he demonstrates how, while his daughter, Diane, and grandson enjoy the ride.

The House of the Future, installed in 1957, demonstrates Walt's commitment to the daily lives of his visitors. In the future, he hoped, monorails, plastics, electronics and American ingenuity would create a better life for everybody.

LAND OF

And if they were wrong, the place looked silly. Tomorrowland presented a serious economic problem, too. The past might need minor revisions from year to year. Fantasy was timeless. But the plussing of Tomorrowland was a constant worry and a major expense. Where the future was concerned, nothing ever stayed the same for long.

One of those plusses was the House of the Future, unveiled in 1957. Designed in a three-way partnership between MIT, a group of architects and the plastics division of Monsanto Chemical, the house resembled a cluster of TV sets mounted on a stalk, like some enormous Martian plant. And almost everything was made out of plastic, from the fiberglass exterior walls to the glowing ceiling panels and the "Atoms for Living"

TOMORROW

LAND OF
TOMORROW

A 1954 layout for what was then called the "Land of Tomorrow" gives special prominence to a monorail system, eventually added to the Park in 1959. Much of Disneyland was devoted to spotlighting pedestrianism and public transportation. Meanwhile, outside the berm, the Age of the Tailfin was in full swing.

kitchen, in which appliances appeared and disappeared with the touch of a finger, the dishwasher manufactured new dishes out of the detritus of the last meal, and the vacuum cleaner scooted around on its own initiative and then put itself away. Every product used in the construction had a zippy, space age name, too. Polyflex. Nytron. Resinox. The list reads like a script for a Superman comic book.

The house is important because it was such a popular Disneyland attraction; it is estimated that 20 million people toured the building during the decade in which it stood close by the entrance to Tomorrowland. During the 1950s and '60s, there was considerable resistance to so-called "modern architecture" of right angles and sparse decor. Or, if modern was what the developer built, then the homeowner was apt to add a Cape Cod gable, a set of shutters and a living room full of maple Colonial furniture. If the Monsanto House did not banish the taste for the cozy, it did inspire interest in the creature comforts that technology had supplied, in the form of plumbing fixtures, kitchen cabinetry and washable surfaces. The House of the Future was reassuring also. By the end of the 1950s, the Russians had launched Sputnik. By the end of the 1960s,

John Hench and Herb Ryman's 1965 design for Space Mountain—an indoor roller coaster specifically intended to satisfy teenagers— finally opened in 1977.

Transportation of Tomorrow

Walt Disney put great faith in transportation systems as a key to America's future. After several smaller upgrades, Tomorrowland went through a major facelift in 1967—proudly called "A World on the Move." Central to all of Walt's plans was the innovative Monorail, that had been around since 1959. This sleek, all-electric "Highway in the Sky" was the first operating daily monorail system in the Western Hemisphere. At first circling only Tomorrowland, it was extended to the Disneyland Hotel in 1961—making it a true "commuter vehicle."

Walt had always felt that young children needed a place to practice safe driving, to prepare them for the rapidly growing freeway system in the real world. The Autopia attraction made a splash with the media on Disneyland's Opening Day in 1955, as celebrities like Frank Sinatra and Sammy Davis, Jr., roared past the cameras in their miniature sports cars. But this "Freeway of the Future" did not turn out as Walt had planned. Guests took "demented delight" in chasing and crashing into one another! It wasn't long before things got back under control—aided by the addition of huge, spring-like bumpers surrounding the body of each car.

The WEDway PeopleMover was a brand new transportation system in 1967, promising to whisk guests around the "new land of the future." At six miles per hour, the whisking went pretty slowly. But these electrically-powered trains mounted to a moving platform did offer guests a sneak peek into Tomorrowland's shops and attractions over a nearly mile-long track. Walt incorporated both this lower-speed but continuous system and the high-speed Monorail into his plans for EPCOT, his Experimental Prototype Community of Tomorrow.

The Submarine Voyage was intended as a serious ride that would recreate the journey of the first ship that navigated the North Pole underwater. But to Walt and his Imagineers, an attraction without a show was a missed opportunity. So, as guests peered out the portholes in their descent beneath the North Pole, they not only enjoyed dazzling views of coral gardens—they also encountered whales, sharks, mermaids, lost ships in the sunken city of Atlantis and even a giant squid!

Concept sketch for the new Tomorrowland of 1967, featuring four modes of transportation—the Disneyland Monorail, Autopia, WEDway PeopleMover, and Submarine Voyage.

The Ultimate Tomorrowland

In October 1966—just two months before he passed away—Walt Disney recorded an enthusiastic pitch for his newest and largest project. It was Walt Disney World in Florida, and its central feature was a model city. He called it EPCOT, or Experimental Prototype Community of Tomorrow. This experimental community was laid out on a radial plan, featuring at its center restaurants, entertainment, shops and a 30-story cosmopolitan hotel. Residents traveled into the city center and out to their homes by way of the now-familiar people movers and monorail system.

EPCOT was Walt's optimistic dreams for solving urban problems of the day. He wanted to prove that the cutting-edge technology of large corporations could benefit people in their daily lives. He imagined that this community would hold upwards of 20,000 residents, who would live there on a temporary basis—say nine months—then return to their regular communities. It was, after all, experimental—a place people would want to study as a model for real-life communities.

Who knows how or if this utopian dream would have turned out if Walt had lived to see it through. Disney executives decided to go through with a place called EPCOT—still part of Walt Disney World in Florida. But when EPCOT the theme park opened in 1982, it was more akin to a world's fair than a prototype community.

Walt's vision for a community of the future did, however, live on. In the mid-1980s, Disney executives began making plans to develop an area of land adjacent to Walt Disney World, and decided to build a new town "from scratch." But ironically, although inspired by Walt's ideas for a town of tomorrow, this new community called Celebration actually bears more resemblance to Main Street than Tomorrowland.

Walt Disney pitches his vision for EPCOT (above). A view of the commercial district in Celebration, Florida (below).

If Disney's Imagineers got it right in their Tomorrowland displays, then things looked old-fashioned almost overnight: the future caught up with hypothetical tomorrows with amazing speed. And if they were wrong, the place looked silly.

Neil Armstrong had walked on the moon. Most Americans would not fly into space by 1986, but their lives were changing, day by day, because of postwar technology. Colonial houses had microwaves. Phones came in colors. Cars had fins like rocket ships. TV dinners came ready made in the grocer's freezer. Cakes came in boxes: just add water and stir. Tomorrow had arrived again.

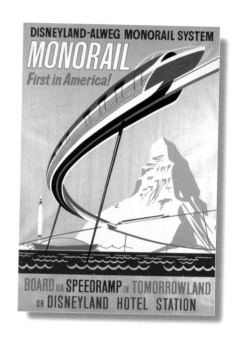

Because of the dilemma posed by representing the future with some accuracy, the shape of tomorrow at Disneyland has changed with dizzying speed. In its most recent iteration, it is the future as Walt Disney and his contemporaries imagined it, with a touch of rock work from one of Lucas' *Star Wars* films. Tomorrow spilled over into Walt's plans to build a real City of Tomorrow on his newly acquired property in Florida. He called it EPCOT: Experimental Prototype Community of Tomorrow. It would have been a functioning urban environment full of People Movers and monorails, manicured green spaces, sub-urbs of modern-style houses with all the latest appliances, and a central skyscraper that was the future's vision of the Sleeping Beauty Castle at the heart of Disneyland. Alas, Walt's EPCOT was never built. The theme park of the same name faces the nagging problem of obsolescence, which can never really be solved. Except, perhaps, by dreaming big dreams and plunging ahead with Walt Disney's appetite for life. For fantasy. For adventure. For history, and for a tomorrow that is sure to be wonderful. ✦

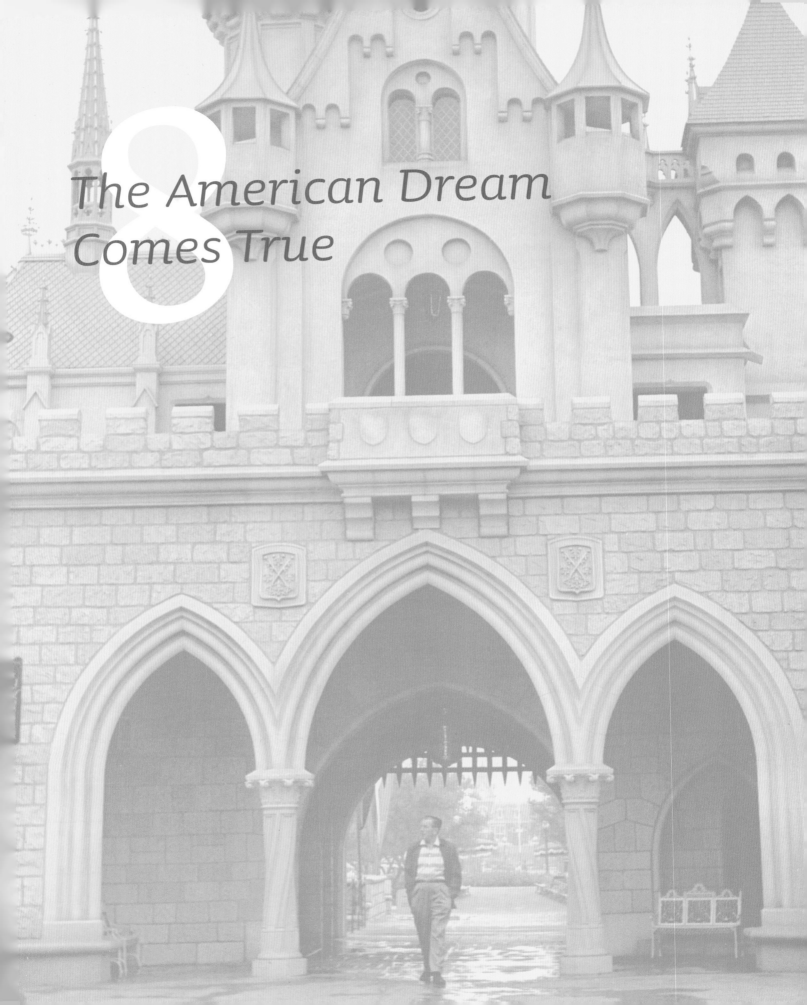

The American Dream
Comes True

8

It is easy to understand why Disneyland was such a hit in 1955—why it rapidly became an American institution beloved by presidents, prime ministers, movie stars and celebrities, and families from every corner of the land. By the end of the first summer of operation, more than a million visitors would pass through the turnstiles and march down Main Street—and they have never stopped coming. They came because Disneyland embodied ideas, yearnings and half-remembered dreams buried deep in the heart of America. Fantasyland reminded us of what it meant to be a child for whom the world is a place of magical happenings often laced with scary moments and moral lessons. Frontierland bespoke freedom, bravery, the errand into the wilderness that once sent the Pilgrims to Plymouth Rock. Adventureland described the mysteries of life in faraway places, filled with strange animals and unfamiliar people. Tomorrowland pointed onward, toward a New Frontier of science, technology and wonders even more magical than those wrought by fairy godmothers. And Main Street reminded us of where we came from—the home towns, the simple pleasures that some of us enjoyed and others conjured up from family stories and the pages of old books.

They came because Disneyland offered a unique opportunity to participate in what had once been the passive experience of moviegoing. Now, anybody could make Peter Pan's glorious flight over London into Neverland, the land that never was. The timid could sit beside Katharine Hepburn on a perilous boat ride into the unknown, with dangers lurking around every bend in the stream. Little girls who almost never

Tomorrowland cast members greet guests (above).

Walt emerges from Sleeping Beauty Castle, August, 1957 (opposite).

First opened in 1955 as "Rocket to the Moon," this attraction was totally re-designed for the new Tomorrowland in 1967. Unfortunately, because the real moon landing occurred in 1969, it soon lost its popularity and was eventually changed to "Mission to Mars."

figured in cowboy movies found themselves stalking the dusty streets of Dodge City or boarding a steamboat bound for New Orleans, just like their brothers did—or John Wayne, Fess Parker, Ava Gardner, Roy Rogers. . . . She could be a spacewoman, boarding a rocket for the moon in far-off 1986, in the company of the famous scientists who talked about the voyage on TV.

Disneyland was television, too—the excitement of sitting in your own living room in Topeka or Buffalo or Boise, in front of your brand new 8-inch screen, and seeing a park grow up in distant, mythical California, land of perpetual sunshine, orange groves, Tar Pits, haciendas and Hollywood stars. Frozen TV dinners sold in the millions because they associated themselves with the new sport of family television-watching: the box looked just like the set, knobs and dials and all. Disneyland carried the same

aura of modern glitz and glamour. It was there, in the picture tube, miniaturized in black and white. But this was no sitcom, no drama. It was colorful and fragrant with the smells of chocolate and coffee and growing things, alive with the sounds of brass bands and roaring lions and distant tom-toms: Disneyland was *real*. Color TV on a giant screen, with you inside!

Disneyland was also the life of Walt Disney, spelled out in buildings and flower beds and ingenious inventions. Main Street came from deep inside his memories of the happiest time of his childhood. Fantasyland came from his full-length animated films, a revolutionary contribution to the movie industry. Frontierland described his influential excursions into Western myth and legend, as a transplanted farm boy half in love with the topography and history of his adopted homeland. Adventureland, plucked

A hit at the 1964 New York World's Fair, the "Carousel of Progress" show was re-installed in this brand-new theater building at Disneyland, which opened in 1967.

Guests view the "Primeval World" from the comfort of brand-new Ford convertibles—part of the Disney-designed "Magic Skyway" show in the Ford pavilion at the 1964 New York World's Fair. Afterward, the Audio-Animatronics® dinosaurs came to Disneyland as a feature on the Disneyland Railroad.

from the Disney documentaries that initially saved the studio from financial crisis, described his travels and interests as well as those of his audience. Tomorrowland was pure Walt Disney, always looking forward, sure that American enterprise would some day change the world. Disneyland was the biography of an extraordinary American who grew up along with the 20th century, and built a place that expressed all its contradictions, imaginings and hopes.

Disneyland has undergone many changes since July 17, 1955. The most important of them came at Walt's instigation. A televised reopening of Tomorrowland on June 14, 1959, was one of his many efforts to plus Disneyland. The trouble with movies, he once remarked, was that when they were done, they were done—warts and all. But Disneyland was like a wonderful toy. He could play with it, fix it, make everything just right. It was utopia in a heart-shaped package. So, while purists jam chatrooms with their objections to the slightest alteration in the Park, Disneyland has reinvented itself constantly, with themed thrill rides for restless teenagers, the always-changing look of Tomorrowland, rides based on new hit films from other studios, and a whole family of attractions originally developed for the 1964 New York World's Fair.

There are other Disneylands today, too, scattered from Florida to Hong Kong. Disney Stores that bring a taste of the Park to the neighborhood mall. Themed hotels, where the park experience spills over into daily life. And untold wonders to come. Disney used to say that it was all started by a Mouse. But it might be more accurate to say that it started with us, with America, and with a man who believed in the stories his country lived by. ✦

*Walt enjoys a walk through
"Nature's Wonderland," along the
tracks of the Disneyland Railroad.*

Tokyo Disneyland was the first Disney theme park constructed outside the
United States (1983). While there are definite differences, some key features of
this Park bear resemblance to the original Disneyland in Anaheim, California.

Image Credits

All original concept art © Disney, Walt Disney Imagineering ART COLLECTION. Property of Walt Disney Imagineering.

2 & 65 (top): Exterior Elevation, Snow White's Adventures, by Eyvind Earle, 1954

11 & 33: Pencil Sketch, Disneyland, by Herb Ryman, September 28, 1953

28–29: Disneyland Overall by Peter Ellenshaw, 1954

38–39: Main Street, by Herb Ryman, 1954

38 (bottom): Poster Screen Print, "Santa Fe & Disneyland R.R./Main Street" by Bjorn Aronson, 1955

40: Presentation Book, Disneyland Entrance, unknown artist, 1954

41: Exterior Elevation Early Concept, Main Street, by Dale Hennesy, 1953

42 (top): Birdseye View, Edison Square, by Herb Ryman, circa 1954; 42 (bottom): Poster Screen Print, "Carousel of Progress," unknown artist, 1965

48 (top): Presentation Book Concept Art, Liberty Street, by Herb Ryman, circa 1956; 48 (middle): Architectural Concept, Mr. Lincoln on Stage at New York World's Fair, by Sam McKim, May 13, 1963

49: Screen Print, "Red Wagon Inn/Main Street," unknown artist, 1955

52: Screen Print, "Mad Tea Party/Dumbo/Carousel/Fantasyland," by Bjorn Aronson, 1955

53: Screen Print, "Alice in Wonderland/Fantasyland," unknown artist, 1958

54: Peter Pan Fly-Through, by Bill Martin, 1954

55: Toy Shop, by Roy Rulin, 1954

56–57 (top): Early Concepts, King Arthur Carrousel, Casey Jr. Circus Train, Peter Pan's Flight, Snow White's Adventures, by Bruce Bushman, 1954; 56–57 (bottom): Early Concepts, Storybook Land Canal Boats, Duck Bumps, Dumbo the Flying Elephant, Mad Tea Party, by Bruce Bushman, 1954

58 (top): Color concept for Castle at Disneyland Paris, "Le Chateau de la Belle Au Bois Dormant," by Vally Mestroni & Crystal Speck, December 22, 1997; 58 (bottom): Suggestion for Lighting the Central Plaza, by Herb Ryman, Christmas Season 1955

60–61: Concept Art, Sleeping Beauty Castle, by Herb Ryman, 1954

62: North Pole Eskimos, "it's a small world," 1964 New York World's Fair, by Mary Blair, 1963

63 (top): Show Scene, Europe, "it's a small world," by Mary Blair, 1963

65 (center): Exterior Elevation, Storybook Land Canal Boats, Geppeto Village, unknown artist, circa 1953; 65 (bottom): Exterior Overall, Toad Hall, Mr. Toad's Wild Ride, by David Negron, June 1982

69 (top left): Poster Screen Print, Mark Twain Steamboat, unknown artist, 1955; 69 (top right): Poster Screen Print, "Casa de Fritos/Frontierland," unknown artist, circa 1955; 69 (bottom left): Poster Screen Print, "Tom Sawyer Island," unknown artist, 1956; 69 (bottom right): Poster Screen Print, "Stage Coach Ride/Mine Train Ride/Mule Pack Ride/Frontierland" by Bjorn Aronson, 1956

70: Frontierland Entrance, by Bruce Bushman, 1954

71: Frontierland Entrance, by Herb Ryman, 1954

72 (top right): Overall Concept, Tom Sawyer Island, by Art Riley, 1957; 72 (bottom): Map of Tom Sawyer Island, by Herb Ryman, circa 1955

73: Shooting Gallery, by Harper Goff, 1955

74: The Golden Horseshoe, by Sam McKim, 1954

76: Poster Screen Print, Mine Train Through Nature's Wonderland, unknown artist, 1960

77: Concept, A Reel-Ride, by Willis O'Brien, circa 1954

78 (top): Proposed front and side elevations, Haunted Mansion, by Sam McKim and Marvin Davis, 1957; 78 (bottom): Haunted Mansion, by Ken Anderson, 1957

79 (left): "Woman on Tightrope" Stretch Painting, Haunted Mansion, Clem Hall, 1982, after concept by Marc Davis, 1965; 79 (right): "Man on Dynamite" Stretch Painting, Haunted Mansion, Clem Hall, 1982, after concept by Marc Davis, 1965

82: Poster Screen Print, "Jungle River/Adventureland," by Bjorn Aronson, 1955

83: Poster Screen Print, "Swiss Family Treehouse/Adventureland," unknown artist, 1962

84: Presentation Book, Jungle Cruise, by Harper Goff, 1954

85: Overall Poster Comp, Tahitian Terrace, by Paul Hartley, circa 1962

86 (top): Interior Elevation, Enchanted Tiki Room, by John Hench, 1962 (repainted by Hench in 1994); 86 (bottom right): Poster Screen Print, "Enchanted Tiki Room/Adventureland," unknown artist, 1963

88: Indiana Jones Adventure, by Chuck Ballew, 1992

89 (top): Dungeon Scene, Pirates of the Caribbean, by Marc Davis, 1965; 89 (middle): Show Scene, Pirates of the Caribbean, by Herb Ryman, circa 1965; 89 (bottom left): Poster Screen Print, "Pirates of the Caribbean/New Orleans Square," unknown artist, circa 1960

92 (top): Poster Screen Print, "Rocket to the Moon/Tomorrowland" by Bjorn Aronson, 1955; 92 (bottom): Poster Screen Print, "Autopia/Tomorrowland," unknown artist, 1960

93 (top): Poster Screen Print, Skyway to Fantasyland, unknown artist, 1956; 93 (bottom): Poster Screen Print, "PeopleMover/Tomorrowland," unknown artist, 1967

94: (right): Poster Screen Print, "Fly Your Own Flying Saucer/Tomorrowland," unknown artist, 1961

96 (top): Architectural Concept, House of the Future, by Herb Ryman, 1956

96–97: Tomorrowland Entrance, by Herb Ryman, 1954

98: Exterior Overall, Space Mountain, by John Hench and Herb Ryman, February 11, 1965

99 (top): Poster Screen Print, "Submarine Voyage/Tomorrowland," unknown artist, 1959; 99 (bottom): Concept Sketch, New Tomorrowland, by John Hench, February 11, 1965

101: Poster Screen Print, Disneyland Monorail, by Paul Hartley, 1959

104: Flight to the Moon, by Herb Ryman, 1967

105: Carousel of Progress, by Collin Campbell, 1966

108–109: Overall View from Hub, Tokyo Disneyland, by Herb Ryman, 1976

All photographs © Disney.

Front cover and 102: Walt Disney at
Sleeping Beauty Castle, Disneyland,
Anaheim, California, August 1957; 14, 15,
18 (inset), 16 & 18, 19, 23, 24 & 26, 25 (inset),
27, 30, 35 (top), 35 (bottom), 44, 46–47, 48
(bottom left), 48 (bottom right): 1983; 59:
1981; 63 (bottom), 68 (top), 75, 87: 1970–1995;
94 (left): 1962–66; 95: 1957; 100 (top), 100
(bottom), 103: 1958–62; 107: circa 1957

From the collections of The Henry Ford.

5: Adult Ticket Book, 1962 [2005.64.1], "E"
Ticket from Child's Ticket Book, 1967–68
[2005.82.5]; 6: [P.188-27455]; 8 (top):
[91.0.44.51]; 8 (bottom): [91.0.44.52]; 10:
[A-8972]; 25: Photoprint, Crosley Custom
television, 1955 [90.1.1746.16]; 32 (top):
[87.9.4.2]; 32 (middle): [Woman's Home
Companion, 1951]; 33 (bottom): [A-19, 1953];
34: Jigsaw Puzzle, Tomorrowland, 1955–60
[2005.83.1]; 68 (bottom): Souvenir Coonskin
Cap, 1958–60 [86.118.1, gift of William S.
Pretzer]; 86 (bottom left): Souvenir Tiki Salt
& Pepper Shakers, 1963–70 [2005.50.1]; 106:
[P.0-7333]

Loans to the "Behind the Magic—50 Years of
Disneyland" exhibition.

12, 16–17, 36–37, 50–51, 66–67, 80–81, 90–91:
Brochure, "The Story of Disneyland," 1955
[Anonymous loan]; 20–21: Map and Guide,
"Welcome to Disneyland," 1955
[Anonymous loan]; 30 (inset): Hand-tinted
postcard, "Kansas Avenue Looking South,
Marceline, Missouri", circa 1920, Dan Viets,
Private Collection; 35 (inset): Chicago
Railroad Fair Official Guide Book, 1948
[Anonymous loan]

Karal Ann Marling is a tenured professor of art history and American studies at the University of Minnesota. An acknowledged expert in the field of American pop culture, she has had visiting appointments at Carleton College, the Buffalo Bill Center, Cornell University, Harvard University, Catholic University of Lublin (Poland), and Moscow State University (Russia).

Complementing her academic achievements is a distinguished career as an author and journalist. Three of her books—*Wall-to-Wall America: A Cultural History of Post-Office Murals of the Great Depression*; *George Washington Slept Here: Colonial Revivals and American Culture, 1876–1986*; and *As Seen on TV: The Visual Culture of Everyday Life in the 1950s* were named *New York Times* books of the year.

Donna R. Braden has served as a curator and experience developer for The Henry Ford for the past 28 years. She is an expert on American pop culture and American leisure and has extensively researched and studied Walt Disney's theme parks and their connection to the broader subject of American vacations.

Braden's publications include *Leisure and Entertainment in America* and *Old Collections, New Audiences: Decorative Arts and Visitor Experience for the 21st Century*.

Henry Ford Museum®
Greenfield Village®
IMAX® Theatre
Ford Rouge Factory Tour
Benson Ford Research Center™

20900 Oakwood Boulevard, Dearborn, Michigan 48124-4088
Phone 313-982-6001   Web: www.TheHenryFord.org

The Henry Ford Editorial Team: Terri Anderson, Donna R. Braden, Wes Hardin & Toby Hines

Special thanks to Jim Clark, Walt Disney Imagineering

Book designed by Savitski Design, Ann Arbor, Michigan
Printed by University Lithoprinters, Inc., Ann Arbor, Michigan